The

DASH

DIET COOKBOOK

Quick and Delicious Recipes for
Losing Weight, Preventing Diabetes
and Lowering Blood Pressure

Dr. Mariza Snyder, Dr. Lauren Clum and Anna V. Zulaica

Ulysses Press

Published in the U.S. by
ULYSSES PRESS
P.O. Box 3440
Berkeley, CA 94703
www.ulyssespress.com

ISBN13: 978-1-61243-047-8
Library of Congress Control Number 2012930815

Acquisitions Editor: Kelly Reed
Managing Editor: Claire Chun
Editor: Susan Lang
Proofreader: Elyce Berrigan-Dunlop
Production: Judith Metzener
Front cover design: what!design @ whatweb.com
Cover photos: © stopwatch icon © Sodafish/istockphoto.com;
    squash © cstar55/istockphoto.com; muffins © Jacob VanHouten/
    istockphoto.com; salmon © Lauri Patterson/istockphoto.com;
    asparagus soup © nicolebranan/istockphoto.com

Printed in the United States by Bang Printing

10 9 8 7 6 5 4 3 2 1

Distributed by Publishers Group West

NOTE TO READERS
This book has been written and published strictly for informational and educational
purposes only. It is not intended to serve as medical advice or to be any form of medical treatment. You should always consult your physician before altering or changing
any aspect of your medical treatment and/or undertaking a diet regimen, including
the guidelines as described in this book. Do not stop or change any prescription
medications without the guidance and advice of your physician. Any use of the information in this book is made on the reader's good judgment after consulting with his
or her physician and is the reader's sole responsibility. This book is not intended to
diagnose or treat any medical condition and is not a substitute for a physician.

Contents

Acknowledgments 5

Introduction 7

Section One: How the DASH Diet Works 9

Section Two: Using DASH to Lose Weight 21

Section Three: DASH-Friendly Recipes 33

    Smoothies 37

    Breakfast 52

    Lunch 81

    Dinner 122

    Appetizers and Side Dishes 177

    Desserts 214

Section Four: The 28-Day Meal Plan 251

Resources 273

Recipe Index 275

About the Authors 278

Conversions 280

Acknowledgments

I would like to thank all of my friends and family for their continued support and love. I would like to extend a very special thanks to my coauthors, Dr. Lauren Clum and Anna V. Zulaica. I am so proud to work with you. —M. S.

I want to deeply thank all of my family and friends for all of their love and support they have showed me in the process of writing this book. Thank you for being my taste testers and critics! Special thanks to my great friends and colleagues, Lauren Clum and Mariza Snyder. —A. V. Z.

I would like to recognize all of my family, friends, and patients for their contributions to my development as a chiropractor, educator, author, and person. A very special thanks goes to my husband, Paul, for his unwavering support and confidence in me, and to my amazing coauthors, Dr. Mariza Snyder and chef Anna V. Zulaica, for their continued passion and commitment. —L. C.

Introduction

DASH is a user-friendly, well-balanced way of eating that offers a ton of great choices. The recipes in this book focus on fresh, whole ingredients so that the transition to DASH is easy and delicious.

The DASH eating plan was originally developed to prevent hypertension (high blood pressure) through dietary recommendations of the National Heart, Lung, and Blood Institute, an institute of the National Institutes of Health. In fact, "DASH" stands for "Dietary Approaches to Stop Hypertension." These heart-healthy guidelines were designed to minimize the intake of processed sugars, salt, cholesterol, and saturated fats while increasing the intake of nutrient-rich foods with the aim of lowering blood pressure, decreasing weight, and reducing the incidence of chronic disease. The main nutrients DASH focuses on include minerals (such as calcium, magnesium, and potassium), antioxidants, lean protein, and fiber (both soluble and insoluble). When the intake of these key nutrients increases, the body is better equipped to function optimally and to burn calories rather than store them as fat.

In 2011, DASH was rated the best overall diet in the *U.S. News & World Report* annual survey of diets. Twenty-two leading experts in weight loss, nutrition, diabetes, and heart disease analyzed the 20 most popular diets in the United States in these categories: short- and long-term weight loss, nutritional completeness, user friendliness, safety, and ability to prevent or manage heart disease and diabetes. Overall, DASH was rated number one for its effectiveness in battling heart disease and in weight loss while being safe and easy to follow. It was also rated the best plan for avoiding diabetes later in life. Research confirms that DASH measurably reduces blood pressure and body weight, particularly when coupled with regular exercise.

Many frustrated and seasoned dieters will admit that dieting is extremely difficult and is often a failed undertaking. Commercial diets are notorious for promising astonishing results in a short amount of time, without much effort or deprivation of unhealthy habits. Rightfully so, people are skeptical about diets, due in part to so many failed attempts.

That's where DASH differs. DASH doesn't make promises. In fact, it's not even really a diet. The word "diet" has come to indicate making some big temporary change in eating in order to achieve some physical change, at which point the "diet" is over. DASH is actually the complete opposite: a long-term approach to eating as a commitment to health. It is an eating plan designed to promote and support healthy lifestyle changes, making weight loss a very nice by-product of the plan! Healthy "real food" guidelines and eating plans allow individuals and entire families to commit to a realistic way of living and eating as a part of daily life. By equipping the body with the right foods to fight off chronic disease and weight gain, DASH helps people achieve great health.

DASH is an effective, easy-to-follow pathway to weight loss and healthy living, and this book serves as a guideline for incorporating DASH recommendations. It explains how the diet works and how to implement it to lose weight, and includes delicious DASH-friendly recipes as well as a handy 28-day meal plan designed to make the diet as simple as possible.

Section One

HOW THE
DASH
DIET WORKS

As DASH gains popularity, experts are studying the effectiveness of the plan. New research showed that the DASH plan lowered blood pressure in just two weeks. In multiple studies, the people experiencing the greatest results on the plan (meaning a significant decline in blood pressure after just 14 days) were those who, before starting the plan, had moderately high blood pressure or pre-hypertension. For people with severe hypertension who were unable to eliminate their blood pressure medications during the studies, DASH helped to improve their response to medication. Additional research demonstrated that DASH is the safest plan for adults and teens to lose weight, and that it helps with cognitive function, decreases incidence of kidney stones, protects from certain types of cancers and chronic health conditions, helps to reduce the incidence of stroke and osteoporosis, and helps to reduce insulin resistance in type 2 diabetes. Bottom line: The research supports the claim that DASH encourages optimal body function.

DASH was thoughtfully constructed by doctors and nutritionists to provide liberal amounts of nutrients critical for optimal body function. Improved function means better internal communication within the body so that each system of the body works properly and is well connected to other body systems. This improved function and communication promotes healthy cardiovascular (heart) and gastrointestinal (digestion) systems and leads to weight management.

These critical nutrients are found in real food, which sounds simple enough. However, many diets promote the use of processed foods, which not only lack vital nutrients but contain numerous artificial ingredients that the body can't easily break down and process. The real-food crux of DASH is a very different yet simple approach: an eating plan that is rich in fresh vegetables and fruits, 100% whole grains, beans, lean meats, and low-fat and nonfat dairy. These real foods have been designed by nature to nourish and fuel the body properly and optimally.

The Basics: Eat Real Foods!

It seems so straightforward: eat real food. However, our society makes it much more difficult than it should be. Real, or whole, food—that is, food found in nature—is the core of DASH.

This emphasis on eating unprocessed food is one of the reasons DASH has been so successful in sustaining weight loss, decreasing hypertension, and preventing diabetes. The DASH Diet is rich in vegetables, fruits, whole grains, and lean meats and dairy, all of which are whole foods. DASH also emphasizes the elimination of all processed foods, particularly those with added sugar, fat, and salt or with ingredients that the body can't easily handle. Processed food is one of the main causes of unhealthy eating, leading to unwanted weight gain and other chronic health issues.

Processed food has become dominant in the typical American diet and has contributed to the rise in chronic health issues and obesity. Because this type of food is so pervasive in supermarkets, it's important to understand how to identify and avoid it. A food is considered processed when it has been chemically altered by additives such as flavor enhancers, colors, binders, fillers, preservatives, and artificial sweeteners. A processed food often contains lots of ingredients, many of which are not easy to pronounce or even identifiable as food. Food from fast food restaurants, gas stations, and mini-marts, as well as many that come in cans, boxes, bottles, and packages, is often highly processed. Many prepared foods, or those that come with sauces or seasoning packets, are also highly processed.

Top 10 DASH Tips

- Get the highest amount of key nutrients by buying foods that are in season. (A farmer's market is the best place to find seasonal produce.)

- Stock your kitchen with healthy convenience foods: cut-up fresh veggies and fruits, hummus and raw nuts.

- Double up on veggies—1 cup of veggies equals two servings.

- Curb your sweet tooth by having fresh berries or other fruit for dessert.

- Make a quick, easy, and delicious snack: organic, low-fat plain yogurt with almonds and fresh fruit. Try Greek yogurt for a thicker, richer experience!

- All nuts are heart-healthy, but make sure they're raw and not roasted or salted. Give your entrée or salad a healthy-fat crunch by adding 1 to 2 tablespoons of raw nuts.

- Stay hydrated. Drink plenty of water throughout the day by keeping a bottle with you at work and in the car, and always drink water with meals.

- Eat the colors of the rainbow at every meal. The more colorful your plate, the greater the variety of nutrients you're consuming.

- No need to skimp on lattes; just make it with 8 ounces of nonfat milk or unsweetened almond milk.

- Green smoothies made with unsweetened almond milk, fresh fruit, and greens are a quick, easy, and delicious way to maximize fruits and veggies at any meal.

What makes the task of identifying a processed food really confusing is the misleading packaging on supermarket shelves that promotes unhealthy items as "whole" or "healthy." For example, packaged foods often proclaim some health benefit, such as "high in fiber" or "fortified with omega-3s," and appear to be a wholesome choice. The reality is that food companies split nutrients in labs and add them to the foods they process so they can market them as healthy. They fortify these foods with nutrients like vitamins, omega 3 fatty acids, and antioxidants as a clever way to sell them. Don't be fooled—these are highly processed products and do not align with the whole food recommendations of DASH. Don't fall prey to food products that make health claims, or pretend to be something they are not.

One of the best ways to avoid getting tricked into buying processed foods is to stay away from the middle aisles of the grocery store, because that is where processed, packaged foods are typically sold. Focus on the periphery of the store, where whole foods—fruits, vegetables, grains, lean meat, and dairy—are found. Or better yet, shop at local farmer's markets whenever possible. The fruits, vegetables, grains, meats, eggs, and dairy products at farmer's markets are typically farm-fresh and in season, meaning little to no processing and great nutritional value.

As you begin to DASH, take a look at what fills your refrigerator, freezer, and pantry, and start phasing out packaged, processed products and add fruits, vegetables, and whole grains to your shopping list. You'll be surprised at how much processed food has sneaked into your kitchen, from preseasoned sauces and dressings to many cereals and junk food. While throwing away all the processed junk and starting with a blank slate can be quite cleansing, it's not necessary if that's too overwhelming for you. Just stop putting these items on your grocery list and stop buying them. The processed items you have will get used up and won't get replenished, and then you'll be DASHing completely. You will regain control of your health by replacing those processed foods in your kitchen with real, whole foods.

The DASH designers understood the important role that healthy, whole foods play in developing a healthy lifestyle. Only through real, whole foods will you ensure the proper balance of vitamins, minerals, and antioxidants to keep you healthy and lean. This book and DASH will equip you with the proper tools, recipes, and nutritional guidelines to make your transition to healthy living easy and fun.

General DASH Guidelines

Food Group	Daily Servings	Serving Sizes	Examples and Notes	Significance of Each Food Group to DASH
Grains	6–8	1 slice bread 1 oz dry cereal* ½ cup cooked rice, pasta, or cereal	100% whole wheat bread, pasta, English muffin, pita bread, bagel, cereal, grits, oatmeal, brown rice, unsalted pretzels, and popcorn	Major sources of energy and fiber
Vegetables	4–5	1 cup raw leafy vegetable ½ cup cut-up raw or cooked vegetable ½ cup vegetable juice	Broccoli, carrots, collard greens, eggplant, green beans, green peas, kale, lima beans, red potatoes, spinach, squash, sweet potatoes, tomatoes, zucchini	Rich sources of potassium, magnesium, fiber, and minerals
Fruits	4–5	1 medium whole fruit ¼ cup dried fruit ½ cup fresh, frozen, or canned fruit ½ cup fruit juice	Apples, apricots, bananas, berries, cherries, dates, grapes, oranges, grapefruit, grapefruit juice, mangoes, melons, nectarines, peaches, pears, pineapples, plums, raisins, strawberries, tangerines	Important sources of potassium, magnesium, fiber, and vitamins
Low-fat or nonfat dairy products	2–3	1 cup milk or yogurt ½ cup cottage cheese 1½ oz cheese	Nonfat (skim) or low-fat (1%) milk, low-fat cheese, low-fat plain regular, Greek, or frozen yogurt, low-fat cottage cheese	Major sources of calcium and protein
Lean meats, poultry, and fish	6 or fewer	1 oz cooked meat, poultry, or fish; 1 egg**	Lean meat, chicken, turkey, or fish; trim away visible fat; broil, roast, or poach; remove skin from poultry	Rich sources of protein and magnesium

General DASH Guidelines

Food Group	Daily Servings	Serving Sizes	Examples and Notes	Significance of Each Food Group to DASH
Nuts, seeds, and legumes	4–5 per week	⅓ cup or 1½ oz raw nuts 2 Tbsp nut butter 2 Tbsp or ½ oz raw seeds ½ cup cooked legumes	Raw, unsalted almonds, cashews, hazelnuts, peanuts, pecans, walnuts, sunflower seeds; peanut or almond butter; black, kidney, garbanzo, or pinto beans; lentils; split peas	Rich sources of energy, magnesium, protein, and fiber
Fats and oils***	2–3	1 tsp butter 1 tsp olive or vegetable oil 1 Tbsp mayonnaise 2 Tbsp salad dressing	Spreadable butter, canola, or olive oil; low-fat mayonnaise; light salad dressing	27% of calories as fat, including fat in or added to foods
Sweets and added sugars	5 or fewer per week	1 Tbsp sugar 1 Tbsp jelly or jam ½ cup sorbet or gelatin 1 cup lemonade	Fruit-flavored gelatin, hard candy, real fruit jelly or jam, maple syrup, sorbet and ices; sugar; avoid artificial sweeteners	Sweets should be low in fat, but not processed

*Serving sizes vary between ½ cup and 1¼ cups, depending on cereal type. Check the product's nutrition facts label and stick with 1 ounce.

**Since eggs are high in cholesterol, limit egg yolk intake to no more than 4 per week; 2 egg whites have the same protein content as 1 ounce of meat.

***Fat content changes serving amount for fats and oils. For example: 1 tablespoon of regular salad dressing = 1 serving; 1 tablespoon of low-fat dressing = ½ serving; 1 tablespoon of nonfat dressing = 0 servings.

Chart reference: http://www.nhlbi.nih.gov/health/public/heart/hbp/dash/new_dash.pdf, modified by authors

DASH Servings per Day		
Food Groups	*1,200 calories per day*	*2,000 calories per day*
Grains	3	4–5
Vegetables	4–5	5–6
Fruits	4	5–6
Low-fat and nonfat dairy	2–3	3
Lean meats, poultry, and fish	3–6 oz	6–7 oz
Nuts, seeds, and legumes	3–4 per week	4–5 per week
Fats and oils	2	3
Sweets and added sugars	0	fewer than 5 per week

Chart reference: http://www.nhlbi.nih.gov/health/public/heart/hbp/dash/new_dash.pdf, modified by authors

Understanding Blood Pressure*			
Top Number (systolic) in mm Hg	*Bottom Number (diastolic) in mm Hg*	*Category*	*What to do** *
Below 120	Below 80	Normal	Maintain or adopt a healthy lifestyle.
120–139	80–89	Pre-hypertension	Maintain or adopt a healthy lifestyle.
140–159	90–99	Stage 1 hypertension	Maintain or adopt a healthy lifestyle. If blood pressure goal isn't reached in about 6 months, talk to your doctor about alternatives, including but not limited to medication.
160 or more	100 or more	Stage 2 hypertension	Maintain or adopt a healthy lifestyle. Talk to your doctor about alternatives, including but not limited to medication.

* These numbers simply serve as a guideline for understanding your blood pressure. Take your blood pressure, or have it taken, several times over the course of several days to determine what your range is.

** These recommendations are simply suggestions to address high blood pressure as a single health condition. Talk to your health care provider so that he or she can take into consideration your entire health picture and make additional recommendations accordingly.

Chart reference: http://www.mayoclinic.com/health/blood-pressure/HI00043, modified by authors

Section Two

USING
DASH
TO LOSE WEIGHT

Unlike plans in other books that line bookstore shelves, this program isn't going to teach you how to "diet." Failed concepts such as nutrient splitting or rapid weight loss have no place in DASH. Long-term weight loss requires lifestyle changes rather than gimmick dieting. The reality is, DASH promotes a healthy lifestyle, and weight loss is a really nice side effect! DASH focuses on food, including fresh veggies and fruits, complex whole grains, healthy dairy, and lean meats in proper proportion to promote satisfaction and heightened energy throughout the day, without the risk of overeating.

There is so much to gain by becoming a DASHer: weight loss, energy gain, and greater resistance to chronic diseases top the list. DASH makes it easy to lose weight and keep it off by teaching how to choose wisely. It's not a matter of simply following a plan, although that will certainly help in the beginning, but of learning how to make healthy choices. Education, along with the tools and resources to take action, allows for realistic implementation of changes and clears the path to goal completion.

The recipes in this book are designed to make cooking healthy meals delicious and simple, without sacrificing favorite foods and flavors. Incorporating exercise into a daily routine will contribute to major, sustainable change. The last section in this book is a 28-day DASH meal plan, which makes it easy to understand the principles of healthy cooking and eating so that habits actually change.

Calorie Needs for Weight Loss

Before beginning a healthy weight-loss program, it's important to have a starting point or baseline. There are several ways to calculate a healthy body weight. Body Mass Index (BMI) is a measure of body fat based on height and weight. The formula for calculating BMI is:

$$\text{weight (lb)} \div [\text{height (in)}^2] \times 703$$

Example: Weight = 165 lb, Height = 5' 8" (68")

Calculation: $[165 \div (68)^2] \times 703 = 25.09$

BMI is not an exact science. Quick and inexpensive, it gives an estimate of body fat. Generally, the BMI of a person at a healthy weight should fall between 19 and 25.

Waist circumference is another quick way to analyze whether someone is at a healthy weight. Generally, waist circumference should be less than 35 inches for women, and less than 40 inches for men.

Calculating the percentage of body fat is a bit more difficult because it's not something that can be done at home. Technically, body fat is the total weight of a person's fat divided by the person's weight, and consists of essential body fat and storage body fat. The various methods and tools utilized to calculate body fat percentage include (but are not limited to) calipers, infrared light, X-ray absorptiometry, water displacement, bioelectrical impedance analysis, and anthropometric methods. Healthy body fat percentages for adult women is 15 to 22%, and for adult men 8 to 15%.

For ease and convenience, this book advises using BMI to get a baseline. Go to www.nhlbi.nih.gov/guidelines/obesity/bmi_tbl .pdf for a BMI chart. Take a look at the chart, note your starting point, and figure out a healthy goal weight.

Once you have determined your baseline and set a goal, the next step is to determine a time frame for the goal. Healthy weight loss includes shedding 1 to 2 pounds per week. How long will it take to get to your goal?

Now, to start making changes: The nutrition plan is based on 2,000 calories per day, which is meant for people who are physically active. Use the 1,200 calorie per day modification if exercise is not a part of your plan. Do not consume fewer than 1,200 calories per day; the body needs a minimum of 1,000 calories per day for organ function alone. Sometimes decreasing calorie intake to even 2,000 calories a day is too much of a jump for people. In that case, attempt to decrease your daily calories by just 500 per day. If you have no idea how many calories you're actually taking in, then just stick with the 2,000 calorie per day plan, add in more of the healthy snacks that are listed, and work your way down to just 2,000 per day.

DASH Weight-Loss Tips

Gut your refrigerator.   Following DASH requires giving up processed foods and junk. The best way to avoid consuming these items is to get rid of them! Replace the processed foods with real food: fresh fruits and veggies, raw nuts, and whole grains. If it's just too much to toss all the bad stuff at once, then at least stop buying it so that you phase it out of the kitchen over time.

Make a grocery list for the supermarket and farmer's market.   Before you head to the market, have a list of DASH-friendly foods for the weekly meal plans. This preparation helps keep tempting foods at bay. Notice that most of the DASH-friendly foods are located on the perimeter of the supermarket. Avoid the center aisles, where thousands of nutritionally depleted processed foods are found.

Cook at home whenever possible.   Even if it looks healthy, food prepared at restaurants can be filled with lots of extra calories without necessarily providing additional nutrition or satisfaction. There is no way to control the ingredients used or the preparation of food that you don't make yourself. When you cook at home, you have complete control over the type and quality of your food, as well as how it's prepared and how much you eat. It's much easier to read nutrition labels and make healthy choices when you shop for food and prepare it yourself.

Look for DASH foods.   Create a mind-set that seeks DASH foods. Find ways to incorporate fruit into your lunch or dinner. Add a serving of steamed veggies to your meal, and save the rest of the main course for later. At restaurants, order a side of veggies instead of fries. Choose restaurants and cafes that have DASH foods easily accessible to order. Eventually the unfriendly locations will become less desirable.

Stockpile your kitchen and workplace.   Keep your freezer, pantry, and refrigerator filled with DASH foods to avoid mishaps. Keep plenty of freshly cut fruits and veggies along with dairy and nuts on hand for snacks and quick meals on the go. Stock the office fridge, as well, so there are always healthy options available.

Get a handle on portion control.   Our society has turned into a "super size me" world, in more ways than one. Most restaurants serve two to three portions per meal, far more than is needed in one sitting. It's easy to fall prey to this practice at home, too. We

Dash-Friendly Restaurant Tips

• Order a to-go box with your meal, and put half of the food away as soon as it arrives. Once the food is out of sight, you're less likely to overeat.

• Split appetizers, entrées, and desserts with friends and family. Surprisingly, many of the "half" portions are actually regular-sized servings.

• Split a larger salad for dinner.

• Ask restaurants to give you dressing, butter, toppings, and sauces on the side. Eat only a tiny portion of these extras, or none at all.

• Ask the server not to bring bread before the meal. Bread and butter calories add up very quickly. Save calories for the meal itself.

• Eat slowly. Dine with others so that eating alternates with conversation. You'll consume less as you slow down, and you'll have a better handle on when you're full. Drink water throughout the meal to fill up.

• Avoid sugary drinks, including alcohol, with meals. Alcoholic beverages can easily pack an additional 500 to 1,000 calories onto a meal!

• Instead of dessert, opt for a glass of wine or coffee after a meal. There are far fewer calories in these beverages than in a typical restaurant dessert, yet you can still enjoy a post-meal treat.

• Avoid fast food restaurants completely. There is almost always another option. Fast food is laden with processed ingredients and is prepared for quantity, not quality. It's questionable as to whether it's technically real food! Its empty calories lead to weight gain.

get conditioned to large portions and eating too much. We use big plates, bowls, and glassware, and fill them up. To avoid overeating, follow the measurements in the DASH meal plan. Use a digital scale to measure until you understand correct portion sizes.

Exercise

Exercise is an integral component of DASH-recommended lifestyle changes. It will contribute to weight loss, lower blood pressure, and reduced risk of many other chronic diseases such as diabetes and cancer. Making exercise a part of your lifestyle will help you get the results you want to achieve.

Exercise consists of three main components: cardiovascular, strength training, and flexibility. Each component is equally important for burning fat and losing weight by boosting metabolism and increasing muscle mass.

Cardiovascular training strengthens the heart and decreases both systolic and diastolic blood pressure levels. It also speeds metabolism over time, meaning that your body will burn calories faster and more efficiently. Begin cardiovascular exercise slowly and increase the intensity as you build endurance. A great way to start is by walking 30 minutes each day. Walk briskly, increasing your heart rate and breathing rate, to ensure a good workout. (If necessary, begin with just 10 to 15 minutes and work up to 30 minutes.) As your endurance increases, add other cardiovascular activities such as running, stair climbing, bicycling, aerobic classes, hiking, or dancing. Cardiovascular exercise includes anything that involves body movement and that increases heart rate and breath rate. For weight loss, you should perform vigorous cardiovascular exercise for a minimum of 30 minutes at a time, three or four times a week.

Strength training, or resistance training, helps burn fat more quickly by increasing muscle mass and boosting metabolism. Strength training is imperative in order to reach weight-loss goals. Strength training can be done at home, outdoors, or at the gym. As with cardiovascular exercise, start slowly. At first, just use your own body weight for strength training with movements such as squats, lunges, push-ups, and crunches. As your body strength increases, add weights and intensity to workouts. Vary workouts by taking advantage of local resources for weight-training classes, outdoor boot camps, or personal trainers. For maximum weight-loss results, strength training sessions should last at least 30 minutes three or four times a week.

Flexibility workouts focus on stretching and balance. This aspect is often overlooked but is just as important as cardiovascular and strength-training exercise. Stretching helps prevent injury during and after exercise, by allowing muscles and joints to warm up before workouts and recover afterward. Before working out, warm up your muscles for about 5 minutes by actively stretching them. Do big movements, such as arm circles, leg swings, and hip circles, or jump rope. After working out, take 5 to 10 minutes to stretch the muscles you used during your workout session. This type of stretching involves elongating the muscles used during the workout by holding the stretch for several seconds to several minutes. Stretching also provides valuable time to check in with your body and listen to what it needs. Balance exercises help to work tiny stabilizing muscles that influence posture and stability, and include performing exercises on unstable surfaces. One-legged exercises and use of gym balls, foam rollers, wobble boards, and BOSU balls are all examples of balance exercises.

Exercise Recommendations and Guidelines

Five times per week
Cardiovascular   Start by walking for 30 minutes. If you're pushed for time or have any physical limitations, break it up into three

10-minute intervals. Walk briskly so that your heart rate and breathing rate increase. You should feel as if you're working out!

As your endurance improves, vary and increase the intensity of your workouts by incorporating such exercises as biking, running, stair climbing, hiking, swimming, and rock climbing.

Exercise for 30 to 60 minutes for maximum results.

Stretching   Before walking, warm up your muscles and joints by doing arm swings and then leg swings for a total of 2 to 3 minutes.

After walking, stretch by elongating the muscles used and holding the stretch for 1 to 2 minutes for each stretch. Stretching helps prevent injury and promotes flexibility.

Three times a week

Strength training   Focus on training big muscles such as those in the legs, back, chest, and core.

Start with your own body weight for resistance, and then add more weight and intensity as your strength builds.

Do strength-training workouts every other day, resting the big muscles in between workout days.

Balance training   Incorporate balance training into your strength training by utilizing equipment such as gym balls, wobble boards, foam rollers, and BOSU balls and by doing one-legged exercises.

Stretching   After strength and/or balance training, stretch by elongating the muscles used and holding the stretch for 1 or 2 minutes for each stretch.

It's always challenging to begin a new lifestyle habit, such as working out on a regular basis, especially when there are thousands of excuses not to exercise. Here are some tips to keep you on target.

- Get an accountability partner. This person can either work out with you, or just check in with you daily to make sure you're staying on track.
- Write down your goals and see how you're doing every week.
- Keep an exercise journal to record your daily successes and defeats and to monitor your progress.
- Create a routine so that working out becomes a part of your daily activities.
- Save time and money by working out at home. You can create a home gym, or follow workout routines available online, on TV, or on DVD. There are many free resources.
- Work out in the morning, so that you don't run out of time during the day and you start your day energized.
- Take advantage of local resources like classes, boot camps, and personal trainers, so you have an instructor guiding and motivating you.
- Hire a personal trainer to create ideal workouts for you as well as hold you accountable for doing them.
- Create a music playlist that inspires you to work out.
- Invest in workout clothes that make you feel good.
- Always have water with you so that you stay hydrated and energized throughout your workout. (Stay away from sugar-filled or artificially sweetened energy or workout drinks.)

Exercise Log			
Date	*Exercise*	*Start time/ Finish time*	*Notes/Comments*
Monday			
Tuesday			
Wednesday			
Thursday			
Friday			
Saturday			
Sunday			

Caution: If you have hypertension or any other chronic disease, consult your primary care physician before starting an exercise program. Your doctor should perform a physical evaluation of your fitness level before you begin any rigorous activity.

Section Three

DASH-
FRIENDLY RECIPES

Veteran DASHers will tell you that they eat at home more often than not. Cooking for yourself and your family gives you valuable control over what goes into your meals, and makes it easier to make healthy choices. Whenever someone else prepares your food, you no longer know exactly what is in it. You don't know about the quality or freshness of the ingredients, whether they're organic, whether they're processed, or if unhealthy additives are present. You also lose some control over portion size, which is an important aspect of DASH.

There are many benefits to cooking at home for family and friends: it requires you to plan and use healthy ingredients, and to engage with others. Clearly it's impossible to eat every single meal at home, but the more meals you do eat at home, the better you'll stick to DASH and the better results you'll see.

All of the recipes in this book were written and tested by Anna V. Zulaica, chef and owner of Presto! Catering and Food Services, located in the San Francisco Bay Area. As you read through the recipes, keep in mind that you should always use fresh, organic, unprocessed ingredients whenever possible. Salt is kept to a minimum in the recipes ("a pinch," for example, is less than ⅛ teaspoon), and whenever it's included, it's in the form of sea salt, which is less processed than table salt and contains valuable minerals. Nut butters used in the recipes are always the unsalted and raw variety. The texture of the nut butter, whether it is crunchy or smooth, is not specified as it is reliant on your preference. Many recipes include serving suggestions, healthful hints and tips, or recipe alterations. Optional ingredients are sometimes mentioned, but please note that they are not included in the nutrition facts for that recipe. Nutrition facts, listed for each recipe, include information about calories, fats, carbohydrates, sugar, fiber, protein, and the minerals sodium, potassium, calcium, and magnesium.

Smoothies

Smoothies are a quick, easy, and delicious way to fit extra servings of fruits and vegetables into your day, and they're great for on-the-go meals and snacks packed with vitamins, minerals, fiber, antioxidants, and healthy fats. Experiment with different fruit and veggie combinations to find your favorite smoothie!

Smoothie Tips

- Many recipes call for greens. Be sure to blend them with a bit of liquid first before adding other ingredients to your blender, so their fibrous texture breaks down.

- Spinach is the most neutral-tasting green you can add to your smoothie, and it's a good one to start with if you're hesitant about green smoothies. Then experiment with different greens to discover their textures and flavors.

- Some recipes call for fresh fruit, others frozen fruit. Fresh and frozen fruit can be used interchangeably. Just keep in mind that frozen fruit will create a frostier, thicker, colder smoothie than fresh fruit.

- When purchasing frozen fruit, buy organic and avoid added sugar.

- Adding ice is another way to get a thicker, frostier, smoothie.

- Peanut or almond butter, avocado, and coconut oil are healthy fats that you can add to your smoothie. Not only will you feel fuller longer with these ingredients, but the healthy fat helps your body absorb and digest minerals from the veggies.

- Smoothies can be stored in the refrigerator for up to 24 hours. If the smoothie separates into layers during refrigeration, just stir before drinking.

- Always include at least one serving of veggies in your smoothie to ensure that you're getting valuable minerals along with the vitamins in fruit, and to balance the sugary fruit content. (Generally veggies are higher in minerals, whereas fruit is higher in vitamins.)

Blueberry Green Smoothie

Serves 2

2 cups chopped mixed greens (such as kale, collard greens,
  mustard greens, Swiss chard, and spinach)
¼ cup water
⅓ cup chopped carrot
½ cup frozen blueberries
½ cup coarsely chopped unpeeled cucumber
¼ cup unsweetened almond milk
4 ice cubes

Place the greens and water in a blender. Start blending
on low, and as the greens begin to break down, increase
to medium speed until they are completely broken down
and smooth. Add the remaining ingredients, and blend on
medium to high speed until desired consistency is achieved,
about 1 minute. Serve immediately.

Nutrition Facts *(amount per serving)*	
Calories	82
Total Fat	1 g
Saturated Fat	0.1 g
Polyunsaturated Fat	0.4 g
Monounsaturated Fat	0.1 g
Cholesterol	0 mg
Sodium	66 mg
Potassium	516 mg
Total Carbohydrate	17 g
Dietary Fiber	5 g
Sugars	7 g
Protein	4 g
Calcium 14% • Magnesium 10%	

Papaya Goodness
Serves 2

1 cup spinach

1 cup chopped kale

¾ cup water

½ cup chopped unpeeled cucumber

1 green apple, coarsely chopped

1 cup coarsely chopped papaya

1 tablespoon ground flaxseed

Place the spinach, kale, and water in a blender. Start blending on low, and as the greens begin to break down, increase to medium speed until they are completely broken down and smooth. Add the remaining ingredients, and blend on medium to high speed until desired consistency is achieved, about 1 minute. Serve immediately.

Nutrition Facts *(amount per serving)*	
Calories	114
Total Fat	2 g
Saturated Fat	0.1 g
Polyunsaturated Fat	0.2 g
Monounsaturated Fat	0 g
Cholesterol	0 mg
Sodium	32 mg
Potassium	520 mg
Total Carbohydrate	25 g
Dietary Fiber	7 g
Sugars	14 g
Protein	3 g
Calcium 10% • Magnesium 10%	

Wake Up Call!
Serves 2

1 large rib celery, chopped

1 tablespoon fresh parsley

½–¾ cup water

½ cup chopped cooked beets

1 small orange, separated into segments

¾ cup chopped carrot

Place the celery, parsley, and water in a blender. Start blending on low, and as the celery and parsley begin to break down, increase to medium speed until they are completely broken down and smooth. Add the remaining ingredients, and blend on medium to high speed until desired consistency is achieved, about 1 minute. Serve immediately.

Nutrition Facts *(amount per serving)*	
Calories	84
Total Fat	0.3 g
Saturated Fat	0 g
Polyunsaturated Fat	0.1 g
Monounsaturated Fat	0 g
Cholesterol	0 mg
Sodium	178 mg
Potassium	521 mg
Total Carbohydrate	20 g
Dietary Fiber	5.0 g
Sugars	14 g
Protein	2 g
Calcium 7% • Magnesium 7%	

Diabetic-Friendly Green Smoothie

Serves 2

2 cups spinach

2 large kale leaves, chopped (about 1½ cups)

¾ cup water

1 large frozen banana, chopped

½ cup frozen mango

½ cup frozen peach

1 tablespoon ground flaxseeds

1 tablespoon almond butter or peanut butter, optional

Place the spinach, kale, and water in a blender. Start blending on low, and as the greens begin to break down, increase to medium speed until they are completely broken down and smooth. Add the fruit, flaxseeds, and nut butter (if using), and blend on medium to high speed until desired consistency is achieved, about 1 minute. Serve immediately.

Nutrition Facts *(amount per serving)*	
Calories	157
Total Fat	2 g
Saturated Fat	0.3 g
Polyunsaturated Fat	0.4 g
Monounsaturated Fat	0.2 g
Cholesterol	0 mg
Sodium	48 mg
Potassium	807 mg
Total Carbohydrate	35 g
Dietary Fiber	7 g
Sugars	16 g
Protein	5 g
Calcium 12% • Magnesium 17%	

Banana Almond Smoothie
Serves 1

1 large banana

1 cup unsweetened almond milk

1 tablespoon unsalted almond butter

1 tablespoon wheat germ

⅛ teaspoon vanilla extract

⅛ teaspoon ground cinnamon

3–4 ice cubes

Place all the ingredients in a blender. Start blending on low, and as the contents begin to break down, increase to medium speed until desired consistency is achieved, about 1 minute. Serve immediately.

Nutrition Facts (amount per serving)	
Calories	338
Total Fat	13 g
Saturated Fat	1 g
Polyunsaturated Fat	3 g
Monounsaturated Fat	6 g
Cholesterol	0 mg
Sodium	153 mg
Potassium	857 mg
Total Carbohydrate	52 g
Dietary Fiber	8 g
Sugars	25 g
Protein	10 g
Calcium 27% • Magnesium 35%	

Tropical Smoothie
Serves 2

¾ cup frozen mango

¾ cup frozen pineapple

1 small frozen banana, chopped

1½ cups unsweetened coconut milk

½ cup water

1 tablespoon coconut oil

3–4 ice cubes

Place all the ingredients in a blender. Start blending on low, and as the contents begin to break down, increase to medium speed until completely smooth, about 1 minute. Serve immediately.

Nutrition Facts *(amount per serving)*	
Calories	219
Total Fat	11 g
Saturated Fat	10 g
Polyunsaturated Fat	0.3 g
Monounsaturated Fat	0.6 g
Cholesterol	0 mg
Sodium	116 mg
Potassium	362 mg
Total Carbohydrate	30 g
Dietary Fiber	3 g
Sugars	21 g
Protein	1 g
Calcium 1% • Magnesium 7%	

Berry Banana Green Smoothie
Serves 2

2 cups spinach
1 cup water
¾ cup frozen blackberries
¾ cup frozen blueberries
1 small frozen banana, chopped
1 tablespoon almond butter

Place the spinach and water in a blender. Start blending on low, and as the spinach begins to break down, increase to medium speed until it is completely broken down and smooth. Add the blackberries, blueberries, banana, and almond butter, and blend on medium to high speed until desired consistency is achieved, about 1 minute. Serve immediately.

Nutrition Facts *(amount per serving)*	
Calories	159
Total Fat	5 g
Saturated Fat	0.4 g
Polyunsaturated Fat	1 g
Monounsaturated Fat	3 g
Cholesterol	0 mg
Sodium	30 mg
Potassium	522 mg
Total Carbohydrate	29 g
Dietary Fiber	7 g
Sugars	13 g
Protein	4 g
Calcium 8% • Magnesium 13%	

Peach Green Smoothie
Serves 2

2 cups spinach

1 cup water

½ cup frozen strawberries

1½ cups frozen peach

1 small frozen banana, chopped

1 tablespoon coconut oil

Place the spinach and water in a blender. Start blending on low, and as the spinach begins to break down, increase to medium speed until it is completely broken down and smooth. Add the fruit and coconut oil, and blend on medium to high speed until desired consistency is achieved, about 1 minute. Serve immediately.

Nutrition Facts (amount per serving)	
Calories	178
Total Fat	7 g
Saturated Fat	6 g
Polyunsaturated Fat	0.4 g
Monounsaturated Fat	0.5 g
Cholesterol	0 mg
Sodium	27 mg
Potassium	682 mg
Total Carbohydrate	30 g
Dietary Fiber	5 g
Sugars	8 g
Protein	3 g
Calcium 5% • Magnesium 13%	

Green Avocado Smoothie
Serves 2

1 cup chopped kale

¾–1 cup water

1 green apple, chopped

2 small kiwifruit, peeled and halved

1 small avocado, pitted, peeled, and chopped

1 tangerine, peeled and separated into segments

3–4 ice cubes

Place the kale and water in a blender. Start blending on low, and as the kale begins to break down, increase to medium speed until it is completely broken down and smooth. Add the remaining ingredients, and blend on medium to high speed until desired consistency is achieved, about 1 minute. Serve immediately.

Nutrition Facts (amount per serving)	
Calories	271
Total Fat	15 g
Saturated Fat	2 g
Polyunsaturated Fat	2 g
Monounsaturated Fat	9 g
Cholesterol	0 mg
Sodium	29 mg
Potassium	916 mg
Total Carbohydrate	39 g
Dietary Fiber	13 g
Sugars	10 g
Protein	4 g
Calcium 9% • Magnesium 17%	

Melon Mélange

Serves 2

2 cups spinach
½–¾ cup water
½ cup frozen strawberries
¾ cup chopped honeydew melon
¾ cup chopped cantaloupe
1 tablespoon ground flaxseeds
3–4 ice cubes

Place the spinach and water in a blender. Start blending on low, and as the spinach begins to break down, increase to medium speed until it is completely broken down and smooth. Add the fruit, flaxseeds, and ice, and blend on medium to high speed until desired consistency is achieved, about 1 minute. Serve immediately.

Nutrition Facts *(amount per serving)*	
Calories	77
Total Fat	2 g
Saturated Fat	1 g
Polyunsaturated Fat	0.2 g
Monounsaturated Fat	0 g
Cholesterol	0 mg
Sodium	43 mg
Potassium	376 mg
Total Carbohydrate	15 g
Dietary Fiber	3 g
Sugars	7 g
Protein	3 g
Calcium 5% • Magnesium 9%	

Strawberry Cucumber Delight
Serves 2

1½ cups frozen strawberries

2 cups chopped unpeeled cucumber

Juice of ½ large orange

4 mint leaves

¾ cup water

3–4 ice cubes

Place all the ingredients in a blender. Start blending on low, and as the contents begin to break down, increase to medium speed until desired consistency is achieved, about 1 minute. Serve immediately.

Nutrition Facts *(amount per serving)*	
Calories	61
Total Fat	0.7 g
Saturated Fat	0 g
Polyunsaturated Fat	0.3 g
Monounsaturated Fat	0.1 g
Cholesterol	0 mg
Sodium	4 mg
Potassium	398 mg
Total Carbohydrate	14 g
Dietary Fiber	4 g
Sugars	9 g
Protein	2 g
Calcium 3% • Magnesium 7%	

Pumpkin Pie Smoothie
Serves 2

½ cup pumpkin puree

½ large frozen banana, chopped

½ cup water

1 cup unsweetened almond milk

¼ teaspoon ground cinnamon

⅛ teaspoon ground nutmeg

1 tablespoon pure maple syrup

3–4 ice cubes

Place the pumpkin, banana, and water in a blender. Start blending on low, and as the ingredients begin to break down, increase to medium speed until completely broken down and smooth. Add the remaining ingredients, and blend on medium to high speed until desired consistency is achieved, about 1 minute. Serve immediately.

Nutrition Facts (amount per serving)	
Calories	93
Total Fat	2 g
Saturated Fat	0.2 g
Polyunsaturated Fat	0.1 g
Monounsaturated Fat	0.1 g
Cholesterol	0 mg
Sodium	93 mg
Potassium	394 mg
Total Carbohydrate	19 g
Dietary Fiber	2 g
Sugars	10 g
Protein	1 g
Calcium 10% • Magnesium 6%	

Arugula Smoothie
Serves 2

1 cup arugula

1 cup spinach

1–1½ cups water

½ small banana

1 cup chopped strawberries

½ cup blueberries

1 tablespoon coconut oil

1 tablespoon wheat germ

3–4 ice cubes

Place the arugula, spinach, and water in a blender. Start blending on low, and as the greens begin to break down, increase to medium speed until they are completely broken down and smooth. Add the fruit, coconut oil, wheat germ, and ice, and blend on medium to high speed until desired consistency is achieved, about 1 minute. Serve immediately.

Nutrition Facts *(amount per serving)*	
Calories	154
Total Fat	8 g
Saturated Fat	6 g
Polyunsaturated Fat	0.8 g
Monounsaturated Fat	0.6 g
Cholesterol	0 mg
Sodium	19 mg
Potassium	437 mg
Total Carbohydrate	21 g
Dietary Fiber	5 g
Sugars	11 g
Protein	3 g
Calcium 5% • Magnesium 12%	

Breakfast

It's true: Breakfast is the most important meal of the day. Eating a meal in the morning jump-starts your metabolism for the day, and without it, your metabolism will remain sluggish and even slow down. (Your metabolism determines the rate at which you burn calories.) Eating a meal within an hour of waking ensures that your body has the fuel it needs to get going and carry you throughout the day. These healthy, fresh, quick recipes are a great way to start your day, and offer an alternative to smoothies.

Toast with Almond Butter and Banana

Serves 1

2 slices 100% whole wheat bread

2 tablespoons almond butter

1 small banana, sliced

⅛ teaspoon ground cinnamon

Toast the bread, and spread each slice with almond butter. Arrange the banana slices on top, and sprinkle with cinnamon.

Nutrition Facts *(amount per serving)*	
Calories	484
Total Fat	21 g
Saturated Fat	1 g
Polyunsaturated Fat	5 g
Monounsaturated Fat	11 g
Cholesterol	0 mg
Sodium	421 mg
Potassium	402 mg
Total Carbohydrate	56 g
Dietary Fiber	12 g
Sugars	21 g
Protein	19 g
Calcium 9% • Magnesium 8%	

English Muffin with Berries
Serves 1

1 100% whole wheat English muffin, halved

1 tablespoon low-fat cream cheese

4 strawberries, thinly sliced

½ cup blueberries, mashed

Toast the English muffin halves. Spread the cream cheese evenly on each toasted half, and top with the fruit.

Nutrition Facts (amount per serving)	
Calories	231
Total Fat	4 g
Saturated Fat	2 g
Polyunsaturated Fat	0.8 g
Monounsaturated Fat	1 g
Cholesterol	8 mg
Sodium	270 mg
Potassium	348 mg
Total Carbohydrate	43 g
Dietary Fiber	8 g
Sugars	11 g
Protein	8 g
Calcium 5% • Magnesium 15%	

Healthy "Lox" English Muffin
Serves 2

1 100% whole wheat English muffin, halved
¼ teaspoon finely chopped fresh dill
½ teaspoon fresh lemon juice
2 tablespoons low-fat cream cheese
1 (4-ounce) can wild salmon in water, no salt added, drained
6 thin slices unpeeled cucumber
6 thin slices Roma tomato
Cracked black pepper

Toast the English muffin halves. Meanwhile, in a small bowl, mix the chopped dill and lemon juice evenly into the cream cheese. Spread the cream cheese mixture evenly onto each toasted muffin half. Rinse the salmon under running water to remove the canned liquid, and then scoop the salmon evenly onto the English muffin halves. If the salmon is too large, mash with fork first. Top with cucumber and tomato slices, and sprinkle with pepper to taste.

Nutrition Facts (amount per serving)	
Calories	192
Total Fat	8 g
Saturated Fat	2 g
Polyunsaturated Fat	0.5 g
Monounsaturated Fat	0.9 g
Cholesterol	8 mg
Sodium	160 mg
Potassium	241 mg
Total Carbohydrate	18 g
Dietary Fiber	3 g
Sugars	0.1 g
Protein	14 g
Calcium 3% • Magnesium 8%	

Protein Bowl
Serves 1

¾ cup low-fat cottage cheese

½ medium banana, thinly sliced

1 tablespoon almond butter

¼ cup uncooked old-fashioned oats

Mix all the ingredients together in a small bowl, and enjoy immediately.

Nutrition Facts *(amount per serving)*	
Calories	346
Total Fat	12 g
Saturated Fat	2 g
Polyunsaturated Fat	3 g
Monounsaturated Fat	7 g
Cholesterol	7 mg
Sodium	690 mg
Potassium	547 mg
Total Carbohydrate	47 g
Dietary Fiber	7 g
Sugars	8 g
Protein	28 g
Calcium 13% • Magnesium 24%	

Berries Deluxe Oatmeal
Serves 2

1½ cups unsweetened plain almond milk

⅛ teaspoon vanilla extract

1 cup old-fashioned oats

¾ cup mix of blueberries, blackberries, and coarsely chopped strawberries

2 tablespoons toasted pecans

Heat the almond milk and vanilla in a small saucepan on medium heat. Once the mixture begins to simmer, add the oats and stir for about 4 minutes, or until most of the liquid is absorbed. Stir in the berries. Scoop the mixture into two bowls, and top with toasted pecans.

Nutrition Facts *(amount per serving)*	
Calories	261
Total Fat	10 g
Saturated Fat	1 g
Polyunsaturated Fat	4 g
Monounsaturated Fat	5 g
Cholesterol	0 mg
Sodium	115 mg
Potassium	593 mg
Total Carbohydrate	63 g
Dietary Fiber	11 g
Sugars	9 g
Protein	7 g
Calcium 21% • Magnesium 41%	

Apples and Cinnamon Oatmeal
Serves 2

1½ cups unsweetened plain almond milk

1 cup old-fashioned oats

1 large unpeeled Granny Smith apple, cubed

¼ teaspoon ground cinnamon

2 tablespoons toasted walnut pieces

Bring the milk to a simmer over medium heat, and add the oats and apple. Stir until most of the liquid is absorbed, about 4 minutes. Stir in the cinnamon. Scoop the oatmeal mixture into two bowls, and top with walnuts.

Nutrition Facts (amount per serving)	
Calories	377
Total Fat	16 g
Saturated Fat	4 g
Polyunsaturated Fat	9 g
Monounsaturated Fat	4 g
Cholesterol	15 mg
Sodium	77 mg
Potassium	399 mg
Total Carbohydrate	73 g
Dietary Fiber	11 g
Sugars	17 g
Protein	13 g
Calcium 28% • Magnesium 41%	

Energy Oatmeal
Serves 1

¼ cup water
¼ cup low-fat milk
½ cup old-fashioned oats
4 egg whites, beaten
⅛ teaspoon ground cinnamon
⅛ teaspoon ground ginger
¼ cup blueberries

In a small pot, heat the water and milk to a simmer on medium heat. Add the oats, stirring constantly for about 4 minutes, or until most of the liquid is absorbed. Add the beaten egg whites gradually, stirring constantly. Cook for another 5 minutes, or until the eggs are no longer runny. Stir the cinnamon and ginger into the oatmeal mixture, and scoop the mixture into a bowl. Top with berries and serve immediately.

Nutrition Facts *(amount per serving)*	
Calories	270
Total Fat	4 g
Saturated Fat	2 g
Polyunsaturated Fat	2 g
Monounsaturated Fat	2 g
Cholesterol	5 mg
Sodium	250 mg
Potassium	371 mg
Total Carbohydrate	60 g
Dietary Fiber	9 g
Sugars	7 g
Protein	23 g
Calcium 12% • Magnesium 35%	

Anna's Homemade Granola
Serves 12 (Makes 5–6 cups)

3 cups old-fashioned oats
¼ cup flaxseeds
1 cup sliced almonds
½ teaspoon ground cinnamon
¼ teaspoon ground ginger
¼ cup brown sugar
¼ cup maple syrup or honey
¼ cup extra virgin olive oil
½ teaspoon almond extract
1 cup golden raisins
olive oil spray

Preheat the oven to 250°F. In a large bowl, combine the first six ingredients and mix to incorporate well. In a separate small bowl, mix together the maple syrup or honey, oil, and almond extract. Pour the wet ingredients into the dry ingredients and mix evenly with a spatula until there are no more dry spots. Pour onto two greased sheet pans. Bake for about 1 hour and 15 minutes, stirring every 15 minutes to achieve an even color. As you stir, break up chunks of granola to the desired consistency. Remove from the oven, and transfer to a large bowl. Stir in the raisins so they distribute evenly.

TIPS
• If you prefer raisins drier and chewier, add them to the mixture before baking.
• Substitute dried blueberries, cherries, or apricots for raisins for a variety of flavors, colors, and antioxidants.
• Substitute vanilla extract for almond extract, if you like.

- Maple syrup and honey have different flavor profiles but can be used interchangeably in this recipe.
- Store cooled granola in large zip-top bags or glass containers with lids.

Nutrition Facts (amount per serving)	
Calories	262
Total Fat	11 g
Saturated Fat	2 g
Polyunsaturated Fat	4 g
Monounsaturated Fat	7 g
Cholesterol	0 mg
Sodium	6 mg
Potassium	376 mg
Total Carbohydrate	52 g
Dietary Fiber	7 g
Sugars	12 g
Protein	6 g
Calcium 6% • Magnesium 24%	

Warm Quinoa with Berries
Serves 2

1 cup uncooked quinoa

1 cup unsweetened coconut milk

1 cup water

½ cup blackberries

2 tablespoons toasted chopped pecans

2 teaspoons raw honey, optional

Rinse the quinoa (if not pre-rinsed). In a small covered pot, bring the quinoa, coconut milk and water to a boil on high heat. Reduce the heat to low and simmer for 10 to 15 minutes or until the liquid has been absorbed. Cooked quinoa should be slightly al dente; it is ready when most of the grains have uncoiled and you can see the unwound germ. Let the quinoa sit in the covered pot for about 5 minutes. Fluff gently with a fork and scoop into two bowls, and top with blackberries, pecans, and honey (if using).

Nutrition Facts *(amount per serving)*	
Calories	476
Total Fat	17 g
Saturated Fat	0.8 g
Polyunsaturated Fat	3 g
Monounsaturated Fat	6 g
Cholesterol	0 mg
Sodium	94 mg
Potassium	221 mg
Total Carbohydrate	70 g
Dietary Fiber	10 g
Sugars	7 g
Protein	14 g
Calcium 12% • Magnesium 8%	

Fruity Yogurt Parfait

Serves 1

1 cup low-fat plain Greek yogurt

¼ cup blueberries

¼ cup cubed strawberries

¼ cup cubed kiwifruit

1 teaspoon ground flaxseeds or flaxseed meal

½ cup low-calorie granola (or Anna's Homemade Granola, page 60)

Scoop half the yogurt into a small glass bowl or parfait dish. Top with a thin layer of blueberries, strawberries, kiwifruit, flaxseed meal, and granola. Layer the remaining yogurt and top with the remaining fruit, flaxseeds, and granola.

Nutrition Facts (amount per serving)	
Calories	388
Total Fat	212 g
Saturated Fat	5 g
Polyunsaturated Fat	4 g
Monounsaturated Fat	3 g
Cholesterol	10 mg
Sodium	98 mg
Potassium	713 mg
Total Carbohydrate	41 g
Dietary Fiber	7 g
Sugars	17 g
Protein	30 g
Calcium 25% • Magnesium 22 %	

Banana Almond Yogurt

Serves 1

1 tablespoon raw, crunchy, unsalted almond butter

¾ cup low-fat plain Greek yogurt

¼ cup uncooked old-fashioned oats

½ large banana, sliced

⅛ teaspoon ground cinnamon

Soften the almond butter in the microwave for 15 seconds. Scoop the yogurt into a bowl, and stir in the almond butter, oats, and banana. Sprinkle cinnamon on top.

Nutrition Facts (amount per serving)	
Calories	337
Total Fat	12 g
Saturated Fat	3 g
Polyunsaturated Fat	2 g
Monounsaturated Fat	6 g
Cholesterol	8 mg
Sodium	65 mg
Potassium	579 mg
Total Carbohydrate	48 g
Dietary Fiber	7 g
Sugars	11 g
Protein	25 g
Calcium 23% • Magnesium 21%	

Open-Faced Breakfast Sandwich

Serves 1

1½ teaspoons extra virgin olive oil

2 egg whites, beaten

½ cup spinach

Cracked black pepper, to taste

1 teaspoon brown mustard

1 slice 100% whole wheat bread

2 thick tomato slices

1 thin slice low-fat cheddar cheese

Preheat the oven or toaster oven to 400°F. Heat a small nonstick pan on medium heat. Add oil to the hot pan and when the oil is hot, add the egg whites. Scramble the eggs while cooking, then add the spinach and season to taste with pepper. Spread mustard onto the bread, add the tomato and scrambled eggs, and top with cheese. Heat in the oven until the cheese melts, about 2 minutes.

Nutrition Facts *(amount per serving)*	
Calories	286
Total Fat	12 g
Saturated Fat	3 g
Polyunsaturated Fat	3 g
Monounsaturated Fat	6 g
Cholesterol	6 mg
Sodium	515 mg
Potassium	344 mg
Total Carbohydrate	27 g
Dietary Fiber	4 g
Sugars	0.1 g
Protein	20 g
Calcium 15% • Magnesium 15%	

Broccoli Omelet

Serves 1

2 egg whites
1 whole egg
2 tablespoons extra virgin olive oil
½ cup chopped broccoli
1 large clove garlic, minced
⅛ teaspoon chile pepper flakes
¼ cup low-fat feta cheese
Cracked black pepper

Whisk the egg whites and egg in a small bowl. Heat a small nonstick pan on medium heat. Add 1 tablespoon of the oil to the hot pan and when the oil is hot, add the broccoli. Cook for 2 minutes before adding the garlic, chile pepper flakes, and black pepper to taste. Cook for 2 minutes more, then remove the broccoli mixture from the pan, and place in a separate bowl. Turn the heat to low, add the remaining tablespoon of oil and when the oil is hot, add the whisked eggs. Once they start to bubble and pull away from the sides, about 30 seconds, flip the omelet over and immediately scoop the broccoli mixture and feta cheese on one half of the omelet. Fold the omelet over, turn off the heat, and cover the pan with a lid for 2 minutes. Serve immediately.

Nutrition Facts (amount per serving)	
Calories	493
Total Fat	41 g
Saturated Fat	11 g
Polyunsaturated Fat	5 g
Monounsaturated Fat	22 g
Cholesterol	205 mg
Sodium	984 mg
Potassium	368 mg
Total Carbohydrate	6 g
Dietary Fiber	3 g
Sugars	0 g
Protein	29 g
Calcium 23% • Magnesium 6%	

Veggie Frittata with Caramelized Onions
Serves 6

CARAMELIZED ONIONS

1 tablespoon extra virgin olive oil

1 small white onion, thinly sliced

¼ teaspoon brown sugar

⅛ teaspoon cracked black pepper

FRITTATA

2–3 tablespoons extra virgin olive oil

1½ cups chopped zucchini

1 clove garlic, minced

1 cup thinly sliced cremini mushrooms

2–3 tablespoons finely chopped fresh basil

1 tablespoon chopped fresh parsley or 1 teaspoon dried parsley

2 cups spinach

4 whole eggs

5 egg whites

½ cup 1% milk

½ cup shredded low-fat pepperjack cheese

⅛ teaspoon sea salt

Cracked black pepper

Preheat the oven to 350°F.

To caramelize the onions, heat a medium saucepan over medium heat. Add the oil and when the oil is hot, add the onion, sugar, and pepper. Let the onion "sweat," moving it every few minutes to avoid burning, until light brown and softened, about 10 minutes. Turn off the heat and cover the pan until ready to serve.

Start the frittata by heating a large pan over medium heat and then adding the oil. Toss in the zucchini, and cook for about a minute. Add the garlic, and cook 2 to 3 more minutes before adding the mushrooms, basil, and parsley. Cook vegetables for another minute, sprinkle on salt and pepper (the mushrooms will release water and will not brown if you add the salt right away). Mix together, turn off the heat, and add the spinach.

In a large bowl, whisk together the eggs, egg whites, milk, shredded cheese, salt, and pepper.

Spray a 9-inch circular cake pan with olive oil spray. Pour in the sautéed ingredients and then the egg mixture. Place the pan on the middle rack of the oven, and cook for 20 to 25 minutes, or until a knife inserted in the middle comes out clean. (Eggs can overcook quickly, so keep a watchful eye!)

Nutrition Facts (amount per serving)	
Calories	197
Total Fat	14 g
Saturated Fat	4 g
Polyunsaturated Fat	2 g
Monounsaturated Fat	7 g
Cholesterol	135 mg
Sodium	394 mg
Potassium	329 mg
Total Carbohydrate	6 g
Dietary Fiber	1 g
Sugars	2 g
Protein	14 g
Calcium 18% • Magnesium 7%	

Veggie Scramble
Serves 4

1 cup mixed greens (such as collard greens, mustard greens,
   and kale)
¼ cup chopped red onion
¼ cup chopped red bell pepper
½ cup chopped broccoli
2 tablespoons extra virgin olive oil
2 tablespoons water
1 large clove garlic, minced
3 whole eggs
3 egg whites
⅛ teaspoon sea salt
Pinch of cracked black pepper

Wash the greens and pat dry, cut off thick part of stems, and cut the leaves into 1-inch pieces. Chop the onion, bell pepper, and broccoli into small pieces of about the same size.

Heat a large nonstick skillet over medium to high heat and add the oil once the pan is hot. Add the greens once the oil is hot and sauté for about 3 minutes or until the greens start to wilt. Pour the water into the pan, cover the pan with a lid, and steam for 2 to 3 minutes. Remove the lid, add the broccoli, bell pepper, onion, and garlic. Meanwhile, in a medium bowl, whisk together the eggs, egg whites, salt, and pepper. Once the onion is translucent, add the whisked egg mixture. Stir to evenly break up and distribute the eggs. Cook until the eggs are no longer runny but still look a little bit wet, turn off the heat, and serve immediately.

Nutrition Facts *(amount per serving)*	
Calories	145
Total Fat	11 g
Saturated Fat	2 g
Polyunsaturated Fat	2 g
Monounsaturated Fat	7 g
Cholesterol	139 mg
Sodium	178 mg
Potassium	196 mg
Total Carbohydrate	4 g
Dietary Fiber	1 g
Sugars	0.7 g
Protein	9 g
Calcium 5% • Magnesium 3%	

Mediterranean Scramble

Serves 1

2 tablespoons extra virgin olive oil

⅛ cup chopped red onion

1 medium clove garlic, minced

¼ cup sliced red bell pepper

¼ cup rinsed and drained, chopped canned artichoke hearts

2 egg whites

1 whole egg

⅛ teaspoon dried oregano

⅛ teaspoon cracked black pepper

⅛ cup low-fat feta cheese

Heat a small nonstick pan on medium heat. Add oil to the hot pan and when the oil is hot, add the onion and garlic. Cook for 1 minute before adding the bell pepper strips and artichoke hearts. Sauté the vegetables for another 3 minutes, or until the onion is translucent and the bell pepper is softened. In a small bowl, whisk the egg whites and egg, and season with oregano and black pepper. Pour the eggs in and mix them with a spatula. Cook for 3 to 4 minutes, or until the eggs are no longer runny. Remove from heat, top with feta, and cover until the feta starts to melt. Serve immediately.

Nutrition Facts *(amount per serving)*	
Calories	424
Total Fat	37 g
Saturated Fat	8 g
Polyunsaturated Fat	5 g
Monounsaturated Fat	22 g
Cholesterol	195 mg
Sodium	572 mg
Potassium	179 mg
Total Carbohydrate	5 g
Dietary Fiber	1 g
Sugars	1 g
Protein	21 g
Calcium 11% • Magnesium 2%	

Egg Muffins
Serves 6

4 cups chopped spinach

½ cup chopped green bell pepper

½ cup chopped red bell pepper

4 tablespoons chopped green onion, white ends discarded

14 egg whites

3 whole eggs

⅛ teaspoon chile pepper flakes

¼ teaspoon dried oregano

2 tablespoons finely chopped fresh parsley

⅛ teaspoon cracked black pepper

Pinch of paprika

Preheat the oven to 375°F. In a large bowl, combine all of the vegetables, mixing them together evenly. In a separate large bowl, whisk together the egg whites, whole eggs, chile pepper flakes, oregano, parsley, pepper, and paprika. Spray a muffin tin with olive oil spray, making sure to spray the sides, as well. Scoop vegetables into each muffin cup, filling each about halfway. Pour about ⅓ cup egg mixture into each muffin cup, slowly so as not to displace the vegetables. Place the muffin tin on the middle rack of the oven, and bake for 25 to 30 minutes, or until the eggs are no longer runny in the middle. Remove from the oven immediately to prevent overbaking or drying the eggs. Serve warm.

Nutrition Facts *(amount per serving)*	
Calories	93
Total Fat	3 g
Saturated Fat	1 g
Polyunsaturated Fat	1 g
Monounsaturated Fat	1 g
Cholesterol	93 mg
Sodium	181 mg
Potassium	252 mg
Total Carbohydrate	4 g
Dietary Fiber	1 g
Sugars	1 g
Protein	14 g
Calcium 4% • Magnesium 6%	

Veggie Omelet
Serves 1

1 tablespoon extra virgin olive oil

¼ cup coarsely chopped broccoli

2 tablespoons chopped red onion

1 clove garlic, minced

¼ cup chopped zucchini

2 egg whites

1 whole egg

⅛ cup shredded low-fat cheddar cheese

⅛ teaspoon sea salt

⅛ teaspoon cracked black pepper

Heat a medium-sized nonstick pan over medium heat and add the oil once the pan is hot. When the oil is hot, add the broccoli and cook for a minute before adding the onion, garlic, and zucchini. Sauté for 3 to 4 minutes. In a small bowl, whisk together the egg whites and whole egg and season with salt and pepper. Turn heat to low and add the whisked eggs to the pan with the vegetables, making sure to tilt the pan so the eggs evenly cover the vegetables. After 30 seconds, turn the heat off, flip the omelet, and spread the cheese on half of the omelet. Fold the other half over the cheese, and cover the pan with a lid. Let it steam for 1 to 2 minutes, or until the cheese melts. Serve immediately.

Nutrition Facts (amount per serving)	
Calories	279
Total Fat	20 g
Saturated Fat	4 g
Polyunsaturated Fat	3 g
Monounsaturated Fat	12 g
Cholesterol	186 mg
Sodium	580 mg
Potassium	313 mg
Total Carbohydrate	6 g
Dietary Fiber	2 g
Sugars	0.8 g
Protein	20 g
Calcium 12% • Magnesium 5%	

Egg Burrito
Serves 1

1 tablespoon extra virgin olive oil
2 tablespoons chopped white onion
1 clove garlic, minced
2 egg whites
1 whole egg
1 cup spinach
⅛ cup shredded low-fat cheddar cheese
Cracked black pepper
1 100% whole wheat tortilla
¼ cup rinsed and drained canned black beans
1 tablespoon chopped fresh cilantro
¼ cup chopped Roma tomato
1 tablespoon prepared low-sodium salsa, optional

Heat the oil in a medium pan over medium heat. Add the onion and garlic, and cook for about 30 seconds. Meanwhile, whisk together the egg whites and whole egg. Add the eggs, spinach, cheese, and pepper. Cook until the eggs are no longer runny, about 2 to 3 minutes. Remove the pan from the heat.

Warm the tortilla in a flat pan over medium heat. Place the beans in a small pot, and bring to a simmer. Set the warm tortilla on a plate, and spoon the beans into the middle of the tortilla, in a line. Add the vegetable and egg mixture, and top with cilantro, tomato, and salsa (if using). Fold into a burrito, and enjoy immediately.

Nutrition Facts *(amount per serving)*	
Calories	460
Total Fat	24 g
Saturated Fat	4 g
Polyunsaturated Fat	3 g
Monounsaturated Fat	12 g
Cholesterol	189 mg
Sodium	709 mg
Potassium	518 mg
Total Carbohydrate	39 g
Dietary Fiber	9 g
Sugars	1 g
Protein	28 g
Calcium 14% • Magnesium 16%	

Whole Grain Pancakes
Serves 4 (Makes about eight 4-inch pancakes)

1 teaspoon vanilla extract

1 small banana, mashed

2 cups unsweetened almond milk

¼ cup unsweetened applesauce

1¼ cups whole wheat flour

¼ cup old-fashioned oats

2 teaspoons baking powder

¼ teaspoon sea salt

½ teaspoon ground cinnamon

3 tablespoons brown sugar

½ cup chopped toasted almonds or walnuts

In a medium bowl, mix together the wet ingredients. In a separate, larger bowl, mix together the dry ingredients. Add the wet ingredients to the dry ingredients, and mix well until smooth.

Heat a grill pan to medium heat, and then coat with olive oil spray. Use a ladle to pour batter onto the pan, and cook the pancakes 2 to 3 minutes. Flip them when they begin to bubble on top, and continue cooking for about a minute. Remove from the heat, and stack on a covered plate until all the pancakes have been cooked. Serve immediately.

Serving Suggestion: Serve with chopped fresh fruit and 2 tablespoons of maple syrup per serving.

Nutrition Facts *(amount per serving)*	
Calories	301
Total Fat	10 g
Saturated Fat	1 g
Polyunsaturated Fat	2 g
Monounsaturated Fat	5 g
Cholesterol	0 mg
Sodium	483 mg
Potassium	372 mg
Total Carbohydrate	55 g
Dietary Fiber	9 g
Sugars	14 g
Protein	9 g
Calcium 29% • Magnesium 18%	

Healthy French Toast

Serves 4

4 egg whites
1 whole egg
1 cup unsweetened almond milk
½ teaspoon ground cinnamon
1 teaspoon vanilla extract
¼ teaspoon ground nutmeg
½ teaspoon powdered stevia
8 slices whole grain bread (at least ½–1 inch thick)

In a shallow bowl, whisk together the egg whites, whole egg, almond milk, cinnamon, vanilla, nutmeg, and stevia. Soak each slice of bread in the mixture for about 1 minute per side, so the bread absorbs the liquid and flavors. Heat a griddle pan until very hot, and coat with olive oil spray. Place each soaked slice of bread on the griddle pan, and cook about 3 minutes on each side, or until browned and crunchy. Serve immediately.

Serving Suggestion: Serve with fresh fruit, yogurt, or 2 tablespoons maple syrup per serving.

Nutrition Facts *(amount per serving)*	
Calories	305
Total Fat	7 g
Saturated Fat	1 g
Polyunsaturated Fat	3 g
Monounsaturated Fat	2 g
Cholesterol	46 mg
Sodium	438 mg
Potassium	412 mg
Total Carbohydrate	49 g
Dietary Fiber	6 g
Sugars	0.3 g
Protein	15 g
Calcium 9% • Magnesium 20%	

Lunch

The following lunch recipes are chock-full of fruits, veggies, and healthy protein, offering many options for your midday meal. Don't be tempted to skip lunch in an effort to decrease caloric intake! Doing that will cause your blood sugar to plummet and your metabolism to slow down. Eating healthy food at regular intervals ensures even blood sugar and consistent metabolic calorie burning. Finding that you're super hungry by the time lunch rolls around? Make sure you're getting enough protein at breakfast, as well as at lunch.

Insalata di Farro (Farro Salad)
Serves 6

½ cup roasted chopped zucchini (see below)

2 cups Italian semi-pearled farro

8 ounces chopped fresh mozzarella cheese

1 (8-ounce) jar roasted red peppers, chopped

2 tablespoons finely chopped fresh parsley

2 tablespoons finely chopped fresh basil

⅛ teaspoon dried marjoram

Juice of ½ lemon

2 tablespoons extra virgin olive oil

¼ teaspoon sea salt

½ teaspoon cracked black pepper

ROASTED ZUCCHINI

2 zucchini, cut lengthwise into ¼-inch slices

4 tablespoons extra virgin olive oil

4 tablespoons balsamic vinegar

¼ teaspoon cracked black pepper

½ teaspoon dried Italian herbs

To roast the zucchini, preheat the oven to 400°F. Coat a cookie sheet with olive oil spray, and arrange the sliced zucchini on it. Drizzle with olive oil and balsamic vinegar, and then sprinkle with pepper and dried herbs. Place on the middle rack of the oven, and cook until the zucchini starts to wrinkle and is soft to the touch, 8 to 10 minutes.

Meanwhile, bring a large pot of water to a boil, adding a drizzle of olive oil to prevent the farro from sticking. Add the farro to the boiling water and cook 20 to 30 minutes, or until al dente. Strain in a colander and pour the farro into a large bowl.

Mix the roasted zucchini and all other ingredients into the cooked farro. Toss well, and serve immediately. Serving this dish warm will melt the mozzarella, but it can also be served chilled.

HELPFUL HINTS

• Farro is a versatile, easy-to-cook whole grain. Be sure to get the semi-pearled variety, so that it cooks quickly. Otherwise it needs to be soaked overnight.

• If marjoram isn't readily available, substitute oregano, a relative of marjoram.

Personal Note from Chef Anna: The first time I tried farro was when I was in Italy taking a cooking class. I fell in love with the texture and flavor and wanted to share it with others once I came back to the U.S., since it is not commonly used here. This recipe is fresh and the combination of flavors is delicious. My family members are always asking me to make this dish, and it is always a hit at potlucks!

Nutrition Facts (amount per serving)	
Calories	189
Total Fat	8 g
Saturated Fat	4 g
Polyunsaturated Fat	0.3 g
Monounsaturated Fat	2 g
Cholesterol	22 mg
Sodium	757 mg
Potassium	195 mg
Total Carbohydrate	24 g
Dietary Fiber	4 g
Sugars	0.5 g
Protein	13 g
Calcium 26% • Magnesium 5%	

Asian Quinoa Salad
Serves 6

2 cups uncooked quinoa

4 cups low-sodium vegetable broth

1 cup cooked, shelled edamame

¼ cup chopped green onion

1½ teaspoons finely chopped fresh mint

½ cup chopped carrot

½ cup chopped red bell pepper

⅛ teaspoon chile pepper flakes

½ teaspoon grated orange zest

2 tablespoons finely chopped fresh Thai basil

Juice of ½ orange

1 teaspoon sesame seeds

1 tablespoon sesame oil

1 tablespoon extra virgin olive oil

⅛ teaspoon cracked black pepper

Rinse the quinoa (if not pre-rinsed). In a small covered pot, bring the quinoa and vegetable broth to a boil over high heat. Reduce the heat to low and simmer for 10 to 15 minutes or until most of the liquid has been absorbed. Cooked quinoa should be slightly al dente; it is ready when most of the grains have uncoiled and you can see the unwound germ. Let the quinoa sit in the covered pot for about 5 minutes. Fluff gently with a fork and transfer the cooked quinoa to a large bowl, then mix in the remaining ingredients. Cool to room temperature and serve. This dish can also be served chilled.

Nutrition Facts (amount per serving)	
Calories	331
Total Fat	10 g
Saturated Fat	0.7 g
Polyunsaturated Fat	2 g
Monounsaturated Fat	3 g
Cholesterol	0 mg
Sodium	103 mg
Potassium	95 mg
Total Carbohydrate	50 g
Dietary Fiber	6 g
Sugars	7 g
Protein	11 g
Calcium 3% • Magnesium 2%	

Chicken Pasta Salad
Serves 6

8 ounces whole wheat penne pasta

1 (6-ounce) boneless, skinless chicken breast

1 cup halved seedless red grapes

¼ cup walnut pieces

1 tablespoon red wine vinegar

½ cup chopped celery

½ cup low-fat plain Greek yogurt

½ teaspoon cracked black pepper

⅛ teaspoon sea salt

Boil a large pot of water, adding a drizzle of olive oil to prevent the pasta from sticking. Add the pasta to the boiling water, stirring once, and cook 8 to 10 minutes, or until al dente. Strain the pasta.

While the pasta is cooking, trim the fat off the chicken, if any, and cut it into small cubes. Fill a separate, medium pot with water, and bring it to a boil over high heat. Add the chicken cubes (water should cover them), and boil for 5 to 6 minutes.

Drain both the pasta and the chicken. In a large bowl, combine the pasta and the chicken with the remaining ingredients, and mix well. Refrigerate for 20 to 30 minutes before serving.

VARIATION

• Substitute canned wild salmon or tuna for the cooked chicken. Just be sure to look for fish canned in water, not oil, with no added salt.

Nutrition Facts *(amount per serving)*	
Calories	115
Total Fat	4 g
Saturated Fat	0.5 g
Polyunsaturated Fat	3 g
Monounsaturated Fat	0.6 g
Cholesterol	16 mg
Sodium	84 mg
Potassium	165 mg
Total Carbohydrate	11 g
Dietary Fiber	2 g
Sugars	3 g
Protein	10 g
Calcium 4% • Magnesium 7%	

Healthy Italian Pasta Salad
Serves 4

4 cups whole wheat penne pasta
¼ cup toasted pine nuts
2 cups halved cherry tomatoes
1 cup chopped fresh mozzarella cheese
1 bunch coarsely chopped fresh basil
4 tablespoons extra virgin olive oil
Pinch of sea salt
⅛ teaspoon cracked black pepper

Boil a large pot of water, adding a drizzle of olive oil to prevent the pasta from sticking. Add the pasta to the boiling water, stirring once, and cook 8 to 10 minutes, or until al dente. Strain the pasta.

To toast the pine nuts, heat a large, flat pan over medium-high heat. Add the pine nuts, and stir frequently to avoid burning. Toast for about 2 minutes or until the nuts smell buttery and they are light brown on the outside. Remove them from the pan immediately.

In a large bowl, toss the cooked pasta with the remaining ingredients. The warm pasta will slightly melt the cheese.

Nutrition Facts (amount per serving)	
Calories	388
Total Fat	15 g
Saturated Fat	5 g
Polyunsaturated Fat	3 g
Monounsaturated Fat	6 g
Cholesterol	22 mg
Sodium	254 mg
Potassium	72 mg
Total Carbohydrate	45 g
Dietary Fiber	5 g
Sugars	4 g
Protein	18 g
Calcium 27% • Magnesium 6%	

Balsamic Glaze

Makes 6 (2-tablespoon) servings

2 cups balsamic vinegar

In a large saucepan, heat the balsamic vinegar over low heat for 25 to 30 minutes. Just simmer it, and do not let it boil. To test, dip a wooden spoon into the glaze; if you run your finger over the back of the spoon, it should leave a clean line. Cool and store in a squeeze bottle to drizzle on salads, entrées, and desserts.

Nutrition Facts *(amount per serving)*	
Calories	85
Total Fat	0 g
Saturated Fat	0 g
Polyunsaturated Fat	0 g
Monounsaturated Fat	0 g
Cholesterol	0 mg
Sodium	53 mg
Potassium	0 mg
Total Carbohydrate	21 g
Dietary Fiber	0 g
Sugars	0 g
Protein	0 g
Calcium 0% • Magnesium 0%	

Basic Vinaigrette
Makes 6 (2-tablespoon) servings

½ teaspoon Dijon or brown mustard

½ teaspoon reduced-sugar marmalade (any fruit flavor)

¼ cup balsamic vinegar (sweet) or red wine vinegar (acidic)

½ cup extra virgin olive oil

⅛ teaspoon sea salt

Cracked black pepper

In a small bowl, whisk together the mustard, marmalade, and vinegar. Very slowly drizzle in the oil, and continue whisking the mixture together. (Constant whisking emulsifies the oil and vinegar, dispersing the droplets of one into the other and creating a thick dressing.) Add salt and pepper. Store in an airtight jar or container if not immediately using.

Note: It is recommend that the base for the homemade vinaigrette consists of 1 part vinegar or other acid, such as lemon, lime, or orange juice, and 2 parts oil.

Nutrition Facts (amount per serving)	
Calories	170
Total Fat	19 g
Saturated Fat	3 g
Polyunsaturated Fat	3 g
Monounsaturated Fat	13 g
Cholesterol	0 mg
Sodium	62 mg
Potassium	1 mg
Total Carbohydrate	3 g
Dietary Fiber	0 g
Sugars	0.8 g
Protein	0 g
Calcium 0% • Magnesium 0%	

Honey Lemon Vinaigrette
Makes 6 (2-tablespoon) servings

Juice of 3 lemons (about ¼ cup)

1 tablespoon honey

1 teaspoon chopped fresh thyme

⅛ teaspoon sea salt

⅛ teaspoon cracked black pepper

½ cup extra virgin olive oil

In a small bowl, whisk together the lemon juice, honey, thyme, salt, and pepper. Very slowly drizzle in the oil, and continue whisking the mixture together. Store in an airtight container or jar if not immediately using.

Nutrition Facts *(amount per serving)*	
Calories	173
Total Fat	19 g
Saturated Fat	3 g
Polyunsaturated Fat	3 g
Monounsaturated Fat	13 g
Cholesterol	0 mg
Sodium	49 mg
Potassium	15 mg
Total Carbohydrate	4 g
Dietary Fiber	0.1 g
Sugars	3 g
Protein	0.1 g
Calcium 0.1% • Magnesium 0.2%	

Lemon Vinaigrette

Makes 6 (2-tablespoon) servings

Juice of 3 lemons (about ¼ cup)

1 tablespoon Dijon mustard

1 teaspoon chopped fresh parsley

⅛ teaspoon sea salt

⅛ teaspoon cracked black pepper

½ cup extra virgin olive oil

In a small bowl, whisk together the lemon juice, mustard, parsley, salt, and pepper. Very slowly drizzle in the oil, and continue whisking the mixture together. Store in an airtight container or jar for future use.

Nutrition Facts *(amount per serving)*	
Calories	102
Total Fat	10 g
Saturated Fat	1 g
Polyunsaturated Fat	3 g
Monounsaturated Fat	7 g
Cholesterol	0 mg
Sodium	79 mg
Potassium	81 mg
Total Carbohydrate	9 g
Dietary Fiber	3 g
Sugars	3 g
Protein	0.7 g
Calcium 3% • Magnesium 2%	

Garlicky Balsamic Vinaigrette
Makes 6 (2-tablespoon) servings

½ teaspoon Dijon mustard
1 large clove garlic, finely minced
½ teaspoon reduced-sugar raspberry marmalade
¼ cup balsamic vinegar
½ cup extra virgin olive oil
Pinch of dried oregano
⅛ teaspoon sea salt
Cracked black pepper

In a small bowl, whisk together the mustard, garlic, marmalade, and vinegar. Very slowly drizzle in the oil, and continue whisking the mixture together. Add the oregano and the salt and pepper.

Nutrition Facts *(amount per serving)*	
Calories	66
Total Fat	7 g
Saturated Fat	1 g
Polyunsaturated Fat	1 g
Monounsaturated Fat	5 g
Cholesterol	0 mg
Sodium	90.1 mg
Potassium	3.7 mg
Total Carbohydrate	1.2 g
Dietary Fiber	0.1 g
Sugars	0 g
Protein	0 g
Calcium 0.2% • Magnesium 0.1%	

Mexican Summer Salad

Serves 6

3 heads romaine lettuce, chopped

5 Roma tomatoes, chopped

1½ cups sliced unpeeled cucumber

¼ cup very thinly sliced white onion

¼ cup fresh lime juice

⅛ cup extra virgin olive oil

Sea salt

Cracked black pepper

In a large bowl, combine the lettuce, tomato, cucumber, and onion. Pour the lime juice and oil over the salad, and toss well. Season to taste with salt and pepper.

Personal Note from Chef Anna: Growing up, my mother used to make this salad for my sisters and me as a side dish to many traditional Mexican dishes. It is simple, easy to make, nutritious, and versatile.

Nutrition Facts *(amount per serving)*	
Calories	78
Total Fat	5 g
Saturated Fat	0.7 g
Polyunsaturated Fat	0.6 g
Monounsaturated Fat	3 g
Cholesterol	0 mg
Sodium	61 mg
Potassium	405 mg
Total Carbohydrate	9 g
Dietary Fiber	2 g
Sugars	0.2 g
Protein	2 g
Calcium 2% • Magnesium 5%	

Grilled Romaine Salad with Garlicky Balsamic Vinaigrette

Serves 4

2 tablespoons olive oil

1 head romaine lettuce (about 12 leaves)

¼ cup feta cheese

½ cup halved cherry tomatoes

¼ cup chopped walnuts

Garlicky Balsamic Vinaigrette (page 93)

Separate the leaves from the romaine head, and wash and dry them. Heat a grill to medium-high, brush oil on both sides of each lettuce leaf, and place on the grill. Watch carefully and turn often, as the leaves can wilt quickly. Once char marks are visible, remove the leaves and place three leaves on four individual plates. Top the grilled lettuce with the cheese, tomatoes, and walnuts. Drizzle with 2 tablespoons balsamic vinaigrette, and serve.

Nutrition Facts *(amount per serving)**	
Calories	152 (218)
Total Fat	14 g (21 g)
Saturated Fat	3 g (4 g)
Polyunsaturated Fat	4 g (5 g)
Monounsaturated Fat	6 g (11 g)
Cholesterol	8 mg (8 mg)
Sodium	109 mg (199 mg)
Potassium	126 mg (130 mg)
Total Carbohydrate	5 g (6 g)
Dietary Fiber	1 g (1 g)
Sugars	1 g (1 g)
Protein	3 g (3 g)
Calcium 7% (7%) • Magnesium 4% (4%)	

* numbers in parentheses are figures with vinaigrette

Healthy Cobb Salad with Basic Vinaigrette
Serves 4

4 slices turkey bacon

5 cups spinach

1 cup sliced cremini mushrooms

½ cup shredded carrot

½ large cucumber, sliced

½ (15-ounce) can kidney beans, rinsed and drained

1 large avocado, pitted, peeled, and chopped

⅓ cup crumbled blue cheese

Basic Vinaigrette (page 90)

Heat a medium-sized nonstick pan over medium heat, and coat with olive oil spray. Add the turkey bacon, cook until brown, and then flip and continue cooking, 5 to 6 minutes. Remove and rest on a cutting board. Crumble the cooled turkey bacon by hand, or coarsely chop.

Place the spinach on a large serving platter. Then arrange the mushroom, carrot, cucumber, kidney beans, avocado, blue cheese, and turkey bacon in neat rows atop the spinach. Serve with vinaigrette on the side.

HEALTHFUL HINTS

• With its strong flavor, just a little blue cheese goes a long way, which is why a modest amount of this high-fat ingredient is included.

• For variety, substitute feta cheese for blue cheese. It's milder in flavor and considerably lower in fat.

Nutrition Facts *(amount per serving)**	
Calories	232 (402)
Total Fat	14 g (33 g)
Saturated Fat	4 g (7 g)
Polyunsaturated Fat	1 g (4 g)
Monounsaturated Fat	5 g (18 g)
Cholesterol	23 mg (23 mg)
Sodium	612 mg (674 mg)
Potassium	797 mg (798 mg)
Total Carbohydrate	19 g (21 g)
Dietary Fiber	9 g (9 g)
Sugars	1 g (2 g)
Protein	11 g (11 g)
Calcium 13% (13%) • Magnesium 18% (18%)	

* numbers in parentheses are figures with vinaigrette

Pomegranate Salad
Serves 4

4 cups arugula
1 large avocado, pitted, peeled, and chopped
½ cup thinly sliced fennel
½ cup thinly sliced Anjou pears, thinly sliced
¼ cup pomegranate seeds

In a large bowl, combine all the ingredients, adding the pomegranate seeds last. Toss well, and serve with your favorite oil and vinegar dressing.

HELPFUL HINT
• If you have a mandoline, use it to thinly slice the fennel.

Nutrition Facts (amount per serving)	
Calories	106
Total Fat	7 g
Saturated Fat	0.9 g
Polyunsaturated Fat	0.9 g
Monounsaturated Fat	4 g
Cholesterol	0 mg
Sodium	15 mg
Potassium	414 mg
Total Carbohydrate	12 g
Dietary Fiber	4 g
Sugars	4 g
Protein	2 g
Calcium 5% • Magnesium 7%	

Beet and Heirloom Tomato Salad
Serves 4

1 cup cooked, thinly sliced beets

6 cups mixed greens

1 cup green heirloom tomato, sliced and cut in fourths

¼ cup toasted walnut pieces

¼ cup crumbled goat cheese

¼ cup balsamic vinegar

Cracked black pepper, to taste

Prepare the beets by cutting off the green stems and washing the beets. Cut off the very top and very bottom of the beet, and then peel off the thick skin. Place the beets in a small pot with about ½ to 1 cup of water, and steam over medium heat for about 15 minutes. Once cooked, let cool, and then slice and cut each slice into fourths as with the heirloom tomatoes.

Place the mixed greens in a large salad bowl, and top with the beets, tomato, walnuts, and goat cheese. Drizzle with balsamic vinegar, and grind cracked black pepper over the top.

Nutrition Facts *(amount per serving)*	
Calories	168
Total Fat	10 g
Saturated Fat	3 g
Polyunsaturated Fat	4 g
Monounsaturated Fat	2 g
Cholesterol	11 mg
Sodium	257 mg
Potassium	643 mg
Total Carbohydrate	156 g
Dietary Fiber	2 g
Sugars	6 g
Protein	8 g
Calcium 9% • Magnesium 13%	

Greek Salad with Lemon Vinaigrette

Serves 4

4 cups chopped romaine leaves (about 2 large heads of lettuce)

½ cup halved cherry tomatoes

½ cup rinsed and drained, coarsely chopped canned artichoke hearts

¼ cup low-fat feta cheese

1 teaspoon dried oregano

10 black pitted olives, rinsed, drained, and chopped

8 tablespoons Lemon Vinaigrette (page 92)

Combine all the ingredients in a large salad bowl, and toss well. Serve each dish with 2 tablespoons of the lemon vinaigrette on the side.

HEALTHFUL HINT

• Both artichoke hearts and olives often come in very salty brines. Look for those in water instead of oil, with no added salt.

Nutrition Facts (amount per serving)*	
Calories	69 (171)
Total Fat	4 g (13 g)
Saturated Fat	2 g (3 g)
Polyunsaturated Fat	1 g (4 g)
Monounsaturated Fat	0.3 g (3 g)
Cholesterol	2 g (8 g)
Sodium	311 mg (401 mg)
Potassium	255 mg (259 mg)
Total Carbohydrate	7 g (7 g)
Dietary Fiber	3 g (4 g)
Sugars	0.8 g (0.8 g)
Protein	3 g (3 g)
Calcium 10% (10%) • Magnesium 4% (4%)	

* numbers in parentheses are figures with vinaigrette

Caprese Salad with Balsamic Glaze
Serves 6

5 large beefsteak tomatoes, cut into ½-inch slices

1 bunch fresh basil

1 pound fresh buffalo mozzarella cheese, cut into ¼-inch slices

5 tablespoons Balsamic Glaze (page 89)

5 tablespoons extra virgin olive oil

Pinch of sea salt

⅛ teaspoon cracked black pepper

Arrange the sliced tomatoes on a large platter. Top each slice with a large basil leaf and a mozzarella slice. Drizzle balsamic glaze and oil over the platter, and then sprinkle with salt and pepper.

Nutrition Facts *(amount per serving)**	
Calories	334 (419)
Total Fat	24 g (24 g)
Saturated Fat	9 g (9 g)
Polyunsaturated Fat	2 g (2 g)
Monounsaturated Fat	12 g (12 g)
Cholesterol	43.8 mg (44 mg)
Sodium	408 mg (461 mg)
Potassium	70 mg (70 mg)
Total Carbohydrate	11 g (32 g)
Dietary Fiber	1 g (1 g)
Sugars	4 g (4 g)
Protein	19 g (19 g)
Calcium 51% (51%) • Magnesium 5% (5%)	

* numbers in parentheses are figures with glaze

Grilled Tomatillo Salsa
Makes 16 (4-tablespoon) servings

20 tomatillos, husked and washed

½ small white onion, cut into large pieces

1 large whole jalapeño chile pepper, stem cut off

2 cloves garlic

¾ cup fresh cilantro

1 cup water

½ teaspoon sea salt

Heat a grill to medium-high heat. Place the whole tomatillos directly on the grill. Watch them carefully, rotating every 2 to 3 minutes and turning over to blacken on all sides. It's okay if they blacken or burn, as it will add to their flavor. They're done when they feel soft and squishy when picked up with tongs. Place cooked tomatillos in a pot and cover, so they continue steaming while the rest of the tomatillos finish grilling. Once all the tomatillos have been grilled, leave them in the covered pot for 15 to 20 minutes, until completely cooled. They will release liquid while they cool, which can be used in place of water or mixed with water, to make the salsa.

In a small pot over high heat, cook the onion, chile pepper, and garlic until they start to brown. After 2 minutes, add the tomatillo liquid or mix of liquid and water, and cover. Simmer for about 5 minutes, or until a fork easily inserts into the onion. Transfer the onion mixture, tomatillos (first removing any hard cores and leaving skin on), and cilantro in batches to a blender, and blend on low speed and then high until smooth. Salt each batch to taste. Store blended batches in an airtight container.

HELPFUL HINT

• This salsa is mild enough to use as a sauce over chicken, enchiladas, or an omelet.

Nutrition Facts (amount per serving)	
Calories	15.4
Total Fat	0.4 g
Saturated Fat	0.1 g
Polyunsaturated Fat	0.2 g
Monounsaturated Fat	0.1 g
Cholesterol	0 mg
Sodium	1 mg
Potassium	119 mg
Total Carbohydrate	3 g
Dietary Fiber	0.9 g
Sugars	2 g
Protein	0.5 g
Calcium 0.6% • Magnesium 2%	

Red Mexican Salsa

Makes 12 (2-tablespoon) servings

20 dried red chiles/chiles de arbol

1 large clove garlic

½ white onion, cut into large pieces

2 large Roma tomatoes, cut into large pieces

½ cup water

¾ cup fresh cilantro

¼ teaspoon sea salt

Heat a large skillet over high heat. Add the chiles, garlic, onion, and tomatoes directly to the pan with no oil. Once the tomato skins and chiles start to blacken, remove the chiles from the skillet and place them in a small pot with the water. Cover, and simmer for 8 to 10 minutes to soften the chiles. Once the chiles are softened, transfer the cooked ingredients along with the cilantro to a blender. Blend on low speed, and cover the top with a kitchen towel so that steam can escape, but the salsa won't explode out the top of the blender. Season with salt to taste. Caution: This salsa is very spicy!

Nutrition Facts (amount per serving)	
Calories	10
Total Fat	0.1 g
Saturated Fat	0 g
Polyunsaturated Fat	0 g
Monounsaturated Fat	0 g
Cholesterol	0 mg
Sodium	132 mg
Potassium	54 mg
Total Carbohydrate	2 g
Dietary Fiber	0.3 g
Sugars	0 g
Protein	0.2 g
Calcium 0.6% • Magnesium 0.7%	

Grilled Chicken with Black Bean Salsa

Serves 4

2 cups rinsed and drained canned black beans

1 large Granny Smith apple, chopped

½ small red onion, finely chopped

1 serrano chile pepper, seeded and finely chopped

2 tablespoons chopped fresh cilantro

Juice of 1 large lime

Juice of ½ orange

⅛ teaspoon sea salt

⅛ teaspoon cracked black pepper

4 boneless, skinless chicken breasts

To make the salsa, combine all the ingredients (except the salt, pepper, and chicken) in a large bowl. Refrigerate for at least an hour to let the flavors meld.

Heat a grill or grill pan to medium-high heat. Season the chicken breasts with salt and pepper. Place them on the grill, and cook 4 to 6 minutes per side, or until the center of each is no longer pink. Divide the salsa on top of the breasts, and serve.

Nutrition Facts *(amount per serving)*	
Calories	251
Total Fat	1 g
Saturated Fat	0.2 g
Polyunsaturated Fat	0.3 g
Monounsaturated Fat	0 g
Cholesterol	55 mg
Sodium	232 mg
Potassium	431 mg
Total Carbohydrate	30 g
Dietary Fiber	9 g
Sugars	5 g
Protein	31 g
Calcium 4% • Magnesium 17%	

Beef Tacos
Serves 4

2 tablespoons extra virgin olive oil
½ cup chopped white onion, divided
1 cup chopped red bell pepper
1 large clove garlic, minced
½ pound 95%-lean ground beef
½ teaspoon dried oregano
¼ teaspoon cracked black pepper
¾ cup chopped Roma tomato
1 teaspoon chopped jalapeño chile pepper (seeded for less heat)
4 tablespoons chopped fresh cilantro
Juice of ½ lime
8 (6-inch) corn tortillas
4 radishes, thinly sliced

Heat the oil in a large pan over medium-high heat. Add ¼ cup of the onion and the bell pepper and garlic, and cook for 30 seconds. Then add the ground beef, breaking up any large chunks with a spatula. Cook for 5 to 6 minutes, or until the meat is no longer pink. Add the oregano and black pepper while the meat cooks.

In a separate bowl, combine the remaining ¼ cup chopped onion, tomato, chile pepper, cilantro, and lime juice to make a salsa topping. Mix to incorporate evenly, and set aside.

Warm the tortillas in a flat pan over medium heat. Place two tortillas on four individual plates, scoop the beef mixture onto the tortillas, top with salsa and sliced radishes, fold, and serve.

Nutrition Facts (amount per serving)	
Calories	294
Total Fat	13 g
Saturated Fat	3 g
Polyunsaturated Fat	2 g
Monounsaturated Fat	5 g
Cholesterol	33 mg
Sodium	73 mg
Potassium	318 mg
Total Carbohydrate	31 g
Dietary Fiber	5 g
Sugars	2 g
Protein	16 g
Calcium 8% • Magnesium 1%	

Curried Chicken Salad Pita Sandwich
Serves 4

2 (6-ounce) boneless, skinless chicken breasts

½ cup chopped carrot

⅓ cup chopped green onion

¼ cup golden raisins

¾ cup low-fat plain Greek yogurt

1½ teaspoons red wine vinegar

1 teaspoon curry powder

¼ teaspoon ground cinnamon

4 100% whole wheat pitas (with pockets)

2 romaine lettuce leaves, chopped

8 heirloom tomatoes, sliced

¼ cup chopped toasted almonds

Trim the fat off the chicken, and cut the breasts into fourths. Fill a medium pot with water, and bring to a boil. Add the chicken, and boil 8 to 10 minutes, or until the centers are no longer pink. Strain the chicken, and set it aside to cool. In a medium-sized bowl, combine the carrot, green onion, and raisins. Shred the cooled chicken with two forks, and add it to the bowl. Add the yogurt, vinegar, curry powder, and cinnamon, and mix well. Refrigerate for 30 minutes.

Warm the pitas in a large skillet over low heat, and then cut them in half and split open. Stuff each pita pocket with salad mix, top with almonds, and serve.

Nutrition Facts (amount per serving)	
Calories	340
Total Fat	7 g
Saturated Fat	1 g
Polyunsaturated Fat	1 g
Monounsaturated Fat	3 g
Cholesterol	51 mg
Sodium	297 mg
Potassium	553 mg
Total Carbohydrate	41 g
Dietary Fiber	7 g
Sugars	3 g
Protein	32 g
Calcium 11% • Magnesium 14%	

Chicken Fajita Wraps
Serves 4

3 tablespoons extra virgin olive oil

2 (6-ounce) boneless, skinless chicken breasts

1 teaspoon dried oregano

⅛ teaspoon sea salt

⅛ teaspoon black pepper

½ large white onion, thinly sliced

1 large green bell pepper, thinly sliced

1 large red bell pepper, thinly sliced

4 100% whole wheat tortillas

1 cup rinsed and drained canned black beans

1 cup shredded romaine lettuce

4 tablespoons low-fat plain Greek yogurt

Heat the oil in a large pan over medium heat. While the pan heats, remove the fat from the chicken breasts, slice them lengthwise about ¼ inch thick and cut the longer pieces in half. Season with oregano, salt, and pepper. Add the chicken to the pan, and sauté until the pieces are no longer pink in the center, 5 to 6 minutes. Remove the chicken from the pan, and set aside. Add the onion and bell peppers to the same pan, and sauté until the onions are soft but not completely transparent, about 4 minutes. Warm the tortillas in a flat pan over low heat. Divide the black beans, lettuce, chicken, and sautéed peppers and onions among the four tortillas. Top with yogurt, wrap, and serve.

Nutrition Facts *(amount per serving)*	
Calories	366
Total Fat	14 g
Saturated Fat	2 g
Polyunsaturated Fat	2 g
Monounsaturated Fat	8 g
Cholesterol	35 mg
Sodium	557 mg
Potassium	317 mg
Total Carbohydrate	40 g
Dietary Fiber	9 g
Sugars	3 g
Protein	24 g
Calcium 6% • Magnesium 10%	

Asian-Style Lettuce Wraps with Peanut Sauce

Serves 4

2 cups uncooked red quinoa

4 cups low-sodium vegetable broth

8 large butter lettuce leaves

1 cup chopped snow peas (in thirds)

1 cup bean sprouts

½ cup chopped red bell pepper

½ cup shredded carrot

4 teaspoons sesame seeds

PEANUT SAUCE

1 cup and 6 tablespoons crunchy peanut butter

1¼ cup low-sodium vegetable broth

Juice of ½ lime

½ teaspoon sesame oil

½ teaspoon low-sodium soy sauce

¼ teaspoon ground ginger

¼ teaspoon rice vinegar

¼ teaspoon chile pepper flakes

2 tablespoons chopped green onion, white end discarded

Rinse the quinoa (if not prerinsed). In a large covered pot, bring the quinoa and vegetable broth to a boil over high heat. Reduce the heat to low and simmer for 10 to 15 minutes or until the liquid has been mostly absorbed. Cooked quinoa should be slightly al dente; it is ready when most of the grains have uncoiled and you can see the unwound germ. Let the quinoa sit in the covered pot for about 5 minutes. Fluff gently with a fork.

Place ½ cup cooked quinoa on each lettuce leaf. In a medium bowl, combine the snow peas, bean sprouts, bell pepper, and carrots. In a small saucepan, combine all the ingredients for the peanut sauce. Bring to a simmer over low heat, and stir until the peanut butter dissolves. Pour the sauce into the bowl with the chopped vegetables. Toss well and spoon evenly on top of the quinoa in each lettuce leaf. Sprinkle sesame seeds on top of the veggies, and serve.

VARIATION
• Use ¼ jalapeño chile pepper, sliced very thinly, instead of chile pepper flakes.

Nutrition Facts *(amount per serving)*	
Calories	486
Total Fat	15 g
Saturated Fat	1 g
Polyunsaturated Fat	2 g
Monounsaturated Fat	2 g
Cholesterol	0 mg
Sodium	77 mg
Potassium	135 mg
Total Carbohydrate	73 g
Dietary Fiber	10 g
Sugars	10 g
Protein	17 g
Calcium 10% • Magnesium 9%	

Italian Veggie Pita Sandwich
Serves 1

1 100% whole wheat pita (with pocket)

1 tablespoon prepared pesto

½ cup arugula

1 (¼-inch-thick) slice fresh mozzarella cheese

1 (¼-inch-thick) slice heirloom tomato

¼ cup roasted red pepper (about 2 large pieces from jar)

⅛ teaspoon cracked black pepper

Warm the pita on both sides in a skillet over low heat. Remove from heat, cut the pita in half and split open, and spread pesto on the inside. Fill with arugula, cheese, tomato, and red pepper. Top with black pepper.

Nutrition Facts *(amount per serving)*	
Calories	213
Total Fat	11 g
Saturated Fat	3 g
Polyunsaturated Fat	0.4 g
Monounsaturated Fat	0.1 g
Cholesterol	8 mg
Sodium	379 mg
Potassium	210 mg
Total Carbohydrate	23 g
Dietary Fiber	4 g
Sugars	2 g
Protein	6 g
Calcium 11% • Magnesium 8%	

Turkey Chili

Serves 8

2 tablespoons extra virgin olive oil

½ pound lean ground turkey

½ cup chopped red onion

3 medium cloves garlic, minced

2 cups chopped fresh tomatoes

1 (15-ounce) can garbanzo beans, rinsed and drained

1 (15-ounce) can black beans, rinsed and drained

1 (15-ounce) can kidney beans, rinsed and drained

1 (15-ounce) can white kidney beans, rinsed and drained

2½ cups chopped zucchini

1 tablespoon chili powder

¼ teaspoon ground cumin

½ teaspoon dried parsley

½ teaspoon dried oregano

½ teaspoon dried basil

3 cups low-sodium chicken broth

⅛ teaspoon ground black pepper

⅛ teaspoon sea salt

½ cup shredded low-fat cheddar cheese, for garnish

¼ cup chopped fresh cilantro, for garnish

Heat the oil in a large sauté pan over medium to high heat. Add the ground turkey, onion, and garlic. Cook for 5 to 6 minutes, or until browned, stirring constantly and breaking up turkey chunks with a spatula.

Place the remaining ingredients in a 6-quart crock pot, and then add the cooked turkey mixture. Mix well, cover, and cook on high for 4 hours or on low for 8 hours. Check occasionally and add a little water if the chili becomes too dry. Serve in bowls, and top with cheese and cilantro.

If a crock pot is not available, cook in a large pot with lid on the stove over low heat. Check often and add broth if necessary, as the chili may get hotter and the liquid may evaporate faster on the stovetop than in a crock pot.

Nutrition Facts (amount per serving)	
Calories	266
Total Fat	11 g
Saturated Fat	2 g
Polyunsaturated Fat	1 g
Monounsaturated Fat	4 g
Cholesterol	42 mg
Sodium	497 mg
Potassium	556 mg
Total Carbohydrate	24 g
Dietary Fiber	7 g
Sugars	3 g
Protein	19 g
Calcium 9% • Magnesium 8%	

Vegetarian Chili
Serves 8

3 tablespoons extra virgin olive oil

½ large red onion, chopped

3 large cloves garlic, minced

4 small zucchinis, chopped

½ cup chopped red bell pepper

½ cup chopped yellow bell pepper

2 (15-ounce) cans black beans, rinsed and drained

1 (15-ounce) can kidney beans, rinsed and drained

1 (15-ounce) can garbanzo beans, rinsed and drained

2 (15-ounce) cans low-sodium diced tomatoes

1 tablespoon chili powder

½ teaspoon ground cumin

½ teaspoon dried parsley

½ teaspoon dried oregano

½ teaspoon dried basil

⅛ teaspoon black pepper

⅛ teaspoon sea salt

¾ cup low-sodium vegetable broth

8 tablespoons low-fat plain Greek yogurt

1 large avocado, pitted, peeled, and thinly sliced

4 tablespoons chopped fresh cilantro

Heat the oil in a large pot over medium-high heat, and add the onion and garlic. After 3 to 4 minutes, add the zucchini and bell peppers. Sauté the veggies until the onion is translucent. Transfer to a 6-quart crock pot, and add the remaining ingredients. Cook on low for 4 to 6 hours, adding water if necessary. Serve in bowls, and top with yogurt, 2 slices avocado, and cilantro.

If a crock pot is not available, cook in a large pot with lid on the stove over low heat. Check often and add a little water if necessary, as the chili may get hotter and the liquid may evaporate faster on the stovetop than in a crock pot.

Nutrition Facts (amount per serving)	
Calories	257
Total Fat	10 g
Saturated Fat	1 g
Polyunsaturated Fat	3 g
Monounsaturated Fat	6 g
Cholesterol	0.2 mg
Sodium	426 mg
Potassium	851 mg
Total Carbohydrate	35 g
Dietary Fiber	11 g
Sugars	5 g
Protein	10 g
Calcium 10% • Magnesium 20%	

Kale Vegetable Soup
Serves 6

2 tablespoons extra virgin olive oil

3 medium carrots, sliced

3 small sweet potatoes, diced

1 large yellow onion, chopped

3 large cloves garlic, minced

2 small yellow zucchini, cubed

½ teaspoon dried oregano

¼ teaspoon chile pepper flakes

⅛ teaspoon sea salt

1 quart low-sodium vegetable broth

1 (14-ounce) can low-sodium diced tomatoes

½ teaspoon fresh thyme, chopped

2 cups coarsely chopped kale

1 (15-ounce) can cannellini beans, rinsed and drained

Heat the oil in a large pot over medium heat. Add the carrots, sweet potatoes, onion, and garlic, and cook until they begin to soften, about 4 to 5 minutes. Add the zucchini, oregano, chile pepper flakes, and salt, and cook for 1 minute. Stir in the broth, canned tomatoes with juice, and thyme. Bring to a boil, reduce heat, cover, and simmer for an additional 10 minutes. Then add the kale and beans, and continue simmering until the kale is wilted and the sweet potatoes are soft, about 8 to 10 more minutes. Serve hot.

Nutrition Facts (amount per serving)	
Calories	195
Total Fat	5 g
Saturated Fat	0.8 g
Polyunsaturated Fat	0.9 g
Monounsaturated Fat	3 g
Cholesterol	0 mg
Sodium	297 mg
Potassium	613 mg
Total Carbohydrate	29 g
Dietary Fiber	7 g
Sugars	5 g
Protein	6 g
Calcium 9% • Magnesium 8%	

Tuna Salad
Makes 4 (1-cup) servings

¼ cup chopped celery

½ jalapeño chile pepper, seeded and chopped

¼ cup chopped Roma tomato

¼ cup chopped red onion

2 (6-ounce) cans albacore tuna in water, no salt added, drained

1 teaspoon brown mustard

3 tablespoons low-fat plain Greek yogurt

⅛ teaspoon cracked black pepper

1 small avocado, thinly sliced

In a medium bowl, combine the celery, chile pepper, tomato, and onion. Mix in the tuna, mustard, yogurt, and pepper until well combined. Top the salad with avocado slices, and serve.

SERVING SUGGESTIONS
• Try this salad atop a bed of spinach, and drizzle with red wine vinegar.
• Enjoy it as a dip with whole wheat crackers.

Nutrition Facts (amount per serving)	
Calories	162
Total Fat	7 g
Saturated Fat	0.9 g
Polyunsaturated Fat	0.8 g
Monounsaturated Fat	4 g
Cholesterol	38 mg
Sodium	241 mg
Potassium	318 mg
Total Carbohydrate	32 g
Dietary Fiber	6 g
Sugars	1 g
Protein	21 g
Calcium 4% • Magnesium 5%	

Italian-Style Tuna Salad

Serves 4 (makes 4 cups)

2 (5-ounce) cans albacore tuna in water, no salt added, drained

½ cup chopped Roma tomato

¼ cup chopped red onion

4 tablespoons finely chopped fresh parsley

Juice of 1 lemon

4 tablespoons extra virgin olive oil

⅛ teaspoon cracked black pepper

Place all the ingredients in a large bowl, and stir to incorporate evenly. Let sit for 30 minutes before serving.

Nutrition Facts (amount per serving)	
Calories	205
Total Fat	15 g
Saturated Fat	2 g
Polyunsaturated Fat	2 g
Monounsaturated Fat	10 g
Cholesterol	38 mg
Sodium	192 mg
Potassium	94 mg
Total Carbohydrate	4 g
Dietary Fiber	2 g
Sugars	0 g
Protein	19 g
Calcium 2% • Magnesium 2%	

Dinner

Dinner is easily a favorite meal, offering end-of-day relaxation and connection time with loved ones. These easy-to-follow recipes offer a healthy variety for your evening meal, along with the important balance of veggies and protein. Many can be prepared ahead of time and simply reheated, or are quick to prepare on a week night. And making a little extra can mean lunch for the next day!

Chicken Breasts with Italian Salad

Serves 4

SALAD

1 cup cherry tomatoes, halved

2 small zucchini, sliced thinly and cut into half moons

1 cup diced fresh mozzarella cheese

¼ cup extra virgin olive oil

¼ cup balsamic vinegar

⅛ teaspoon sea salt

Cracked black pepper

4 cups arugula

2 tablespoons chopped fresh basil

CHICKEN

1 teaspoon dried oregano

½ teaspoon minced fresh rosemary

½ teaspoon garlic powder

⅛ teaspoon sea salt

Cracked black pepper

4 boneless, skinless chicken breasts

To make the salad, combine the tomatoes, zucchini, and cheese in a medium bowl. Add the oil, vinegar, salt, and pepper to taste, and mix well. Cover and refrigerate until the chicken is ready. (You'll add the arugula and basil later.)

Trim the fat off the chicken breasts. In a small bowl, combine the oregano, rosemary, garlic powder, salt, and pepper to taste, and mix well. Sprinkle the mixture on both sides of the chicken breasts. Heat a large saucepan over medium heat, and coat the pan with olive oil spray. Once the oil is hot, add the chicken breasts, 2 at a time to avoid overcrowding. Cook each breast 4 to 6 minutes per side, or until the center is no longer pink. While the second batch of chicken is cooking, remove the salad from the refrigerator, add the arugula and basil, and toss well. Once the chicken is done, let it rest for about 2 minutes, and then slice each breast on the diagonal, creating strips of chicken. Arrange the salad on a platter, and top with sliced chicken.

HEALTH TIPS

• Using olive oil spray cuts down on calories and fat without sacrificing flavor.

• Whenever using spice blends, such as garlic powder, be sure to read the label. Many contain monosodium glutamate, or MSG, which is generally recognized as a health hazard. Avoid MSG!

COOKING TIPS

• Adding too much meat to a hot pan at one time will lower the temperature in the pan, and the meat won't cook to a golden crisp. Instead, you'll get steam, which will cook the meat.

• Always let cooked meat rest before cutting it, to avoid releasing juices. Rested meat retains moisture and flavor.

Nutrition Facts *(amount per serving)*	
Calories	400
Total Fat	24 g
Saturated Fat	8 g
Polyunsaturated Fat	3 g
Monounsaturated Fat	13 g
Cholesterol	88 mg
Sodium	549 mg
Potassium	360 mg
Total Carbohydrate	9 g
Dietary Fiber	2 g
Sugars	2 g
Protein	38 g
Calcium 42% • Magnesium 10%	

Orange Chicken and Brown Rice
Serves 2

2 (4-ounce) boneless, skinless chicken breasts

1 tablespoon sesame oil

1 tablespoon extra virgin olive oil

½ cup coarsely chopped shiitake mushroom

¼ cup chopped white onion

1 large clove garlic, minced

¼ teaspoon cracked black pepper

½ teaspoon grated orange zest

¼ teaspoon grated lemon zest

Juice of ½ orange

4 cups spinach

¼ teaspoon ground ginger

1 cup cooked brown rice

Trim the fat from the chicken breasts, and then cut the chicken into small cubes. Heat the sesame oil and olive oil in a medium pan over medium to high heat. Add the mushroom, onion, and garlic, and cook for 1 minute, Then add the chicken, and season with the pepper, ground ginger, orange zest, and lemon zest. Cook until the chicken has browned, about 4 to 5 minutes, and then add the orange juice. Stir the chicken and scrape the bottom of the pan to incorporate flavors. Add the spinach, remove the pan from the heat, and immediately cover it to steam the spinach. Divide the cooked brown rice between two dishes, and top with orange chicken.

Nutrition Facts *(amount per serving)*	
Calories	334
Total Fat	15 g
Saturated Fat	2 g
Polyunsaturated Fat	4 g
Monounsaturated Fat	8 g
Cholesterol	55 mg
Sodium	282 mg
Potassium	498 mg
Total Carbohydrate	25 g
Dietary Fiber	4 g
Sugars	5 g
Protein	27 g
Calcium 9% • Magnesium 20%	

Grilled Chicken Skewers Marinated in Ginger-Apricot Sauce

Serves 4 (Makes about 12 skewers)

4 (4-ounce) chicken breasts, cut into 1-inch cubes

3 large red bell peppers, cut into 1-inch pieces

2 large white onions, cut into 1-inch pieces

6 apricots, pitted and cut into 1-inch pieces

MARINADE

1 heaping tablespoon reduced-sugar apricot marmalade

½ teaspoon sesame oil

1½ teaspoons finely chopped fresh ginger or ¾ teaspoon ground ginger

1 tablespoon Dijon mustard or brown mustard

4 tablespoons apple cider vinegar

¼ cup extra virgin olive oil

1 large clove garlic, chopped

Mix all marinade ingredients together in a large bowl. Place the cubed chicken in a large zip-top bag, pour in the marinade, squeeze the air out of the bag, and seal tightly. Work the mixture into the chicken by hand, by moving the bag and contents around. Refrigerate for at least 2 hours.

Soak 12 large wooden skewers in water, and then chop the peppers, onions, and apricots into similar-sized pieces.

Skewer the pieces of chicken, pepper, onion, and apricot, alternating ingredients. Grill the skewers on a hot grill or grill pan, 4 to 5 minutes per side, or until the chicken is no longer pink in the center. (If using a charcoal or gas grill, close the cover on the grill so the chicken doesn't dry out.)

Nutrition Facts *(amount per serving)*	
Calories	314
Total Fat	16 g
Saturated Fat	2 g
Polyunsaturated Fat	2 g
Monounsaturated Fat	10 g
Cholesterol	55 mg
Sodium	357 mg
Potassium	403 mg
Total Carbohydrate	21 g
Dietary Fiber	4 g
Sugars	10 g
Protein	25 g
Calcium 3% • Magnesium 16%	

Chicken Fajitas with Spicy Avocado Sauce
Serves 4

SAUCE

1 large avocado, pitted, peeled, and cut in fourths

½ cup low-fat plain Greek yogurt

¼ cup water

Juice of ½ lemon

½ small serrano chile pepper

⅛ teaspoon sea salt

⅛ teaspoon cracked black pepper

FAJITAS

4 (4-ounce) boneless, skinless chicken breasts, cut into ½-inch-
thick strips

⅛ teaspoon sea salt

⅛ teaspoon cracked black pepper

1 teaspoon dried oregano, divided

¼ teaspoon ground cumin

3 tablespoons extra virgin olive oil

2 large red bell peppers, cut into ½-inch-thick strips

2 large green bell peppers, cut into ½-inch-thick strips

2 large yellow bell peppers, cut into ½-inch-thick strips

1 large white onion, cut into ½-inch slivers

2 large cloves garlic, minced

8 corn tortillas

For the sauce, place all of the ingredients in a blender and
blend until smooth. Set aside.

For the fajitas, season the chicken with salt, pepper, cumin,
and half of the oregano. Heat the oil in a large pot over
medium-high heat. Once the oil is hot, add the chicken,
and cook 4 to 5 minutes. Add the bell peppers, onion, garlic,
and remaining dried oregano. Season with salt and pepper

to taste, and cook for a few more minutes, until the veggies are soft.

Warm the tortillas in a skillet over low heat. Scoop the chicken and veggie mixture into each tortilla and drizzle with avocado sauce. Fold the tortilla over and serve.

Serving Suggestion: Serve with different toppings such as black beans, shredded lettuce, low-fat shredded cheese, and salsa.

Nutrition Facts (amount per serving)	
Calories	463
Total Fat	20 g
Saturated Fat	3 g
Polyunsaturated Fat	3 g
Monounsaturated Fat	12 g
Cholesterol	55 mg
Sodium	415 mg
Potassium	839 mg
Total Carbohydrate	46 g
Dietary Fiber	10 g
Sugars	4 g
Protein	32 g
Calcium 12% • Magnesium 21%	

Baked Sunflower Seed–Crusted Turkey Cutlets

Serves 4

2 (6-ounce) skinless, boneless turkey breasts

1½ cups unsalted sunflower seeds

¼ teaspoon ground cumin

2 tablespoons coarsely chopped fresh parsley

¼ teaspoon paprika

¼ teaspoon cayenne pepper

¼ teaspoon cracked black pepper

⅓ cup whole wheat flour

3 egg whites

Preheat the oven to 400°F.

Place the turkey breasts in between two sheets of plastic wrap and pound until about ½ inch thick. Cut each pounded breast in half. In a food processor, combine the sunflower seeds, cumin, parsley, paprika, cayenne, and pepper. Pulse a few times, until the seeds are coarsely chopped. Pour the seed mixture onto a flat plate. On a separate flat plate, spread the flour. In a wide, fairly shallow bowl, whisk the egg whites. Set up a dredging assembly line in this order: flour plate, egg bowl, seed mixture plate. Dip each breast into the flour and lightly dredge it on both sides. Then dip it into the egg whites and finally onto the plate with the seed mixture. Press down firmly to coat both sides of the turkey with the seed mixture.

Coat a cookie sheet with olive oil spray, and place the crusted breasts on the sheet. Bake for 10 minutes, turn the cutlets over, and bake for another 10 minutes, or until the thickest part of cutlet is no longer pink in center. Serve immediately.

Nutrition Facts (amount per serving)	
Calories	408
Total Fat	26 g
Saturated Fat	3 g
Polyunsaturated Fat	16 g
Monounsaturated Fat	5 g
Cholesterol	37 mg
Sodium	377 mg
Potassium	467 mg
Total Carbohydrate	20 g
Dietary Fiber	7 g
Sugars	1 g
Protein	29 g
Calcium 4% • Magnesium 16%	

Turkey Meatballs in Marinara Sauce

Serves 4 (Makes about 16 meatballs)

1 pound lean ground turkey

½ small red onion, finely chopped

2 large cloves garlic, minced

¼ cup red bell pepper, finely chopped

3 tablespoons finely chopped fresh parsley

½ teaspoon chile pepper flakes

⅛ teaspoon ground cumin

½ teaspoon dried Italian herbs (premixed, or use thyme, rosemary, oregano, parsley, and basil)

⅛ teaspoon cracked black pepper

1 large egg

¼ cup whole wheat bread crumbs

⅛ teaspoon sea salt

4 tablespoons extra virgin olive oil

1 (16-ounce) jar low-sodium marinara sauce

½ cup low-fat feta cheese

Preheat the oven to 375°F.

In a large bowl, combine all ingredients except the oil, marinara, and feta. Mix well by hand until ingredients are incorporated into the meat, being careful not to overmix. Roll the meat mixture into meatballs the size of golf balls.

Heat a large nonstick skillet over medium-high heat. Once the pan is hot, add the oil and then the meatballs in batches of five. Sear on each side (do not cook all the way through), and place in an ovenproof dish. Once all the meatballs have been seared and placed in the dish, top with the marinara sauce, and cover with foil. Bake for 20 to 25 minutes.

Remove from the oven, and raise the temperature to 400°F. Remove the foil from the dish, top the meatballs with the feta, and bake for 4 minutes. Remove and serve immediately.

Nutrition Facts (amount per serving)	
Calories	546
Total Fat	33 g
Saturated Fat	8 g
Polyunsaturated Fat	4 g
Monounsaturated Fat	14 g
Cholesterol	143 mg
Sodium	1485 mg
Potassium	852 mg
Total Carbohydrate	32 g
Dietary Fiber	6 g
Sugars	2 g
Protein	32 g
Calcium 25% • Magnesium 13%	

Turkey Meat Loaf
Serves 6

1 slice 100% whole wheat bread, crust removed and torn into
  small pieces

¼ cup low-sodium chicken stock

1¼ pounds lean ground turkey

1 large egg

¼ cup finely chopped onion

¼ cup finely chopped bell pepper

¼ cup chopped fresh parsley

1 teaspoon horseradish

1 teaspoon Dijon mustard

1 teaspoon Worcestershire sauce

½ teaspoon sea salt

¼ teaspoon black pepper

Preheat the oven to 350°F. Place all the ingredients in
a large bowl, and mix together with your hands until the
ingredients are evenly incorporated, being careful not to
overmix. Lightly grease a 9- by 5-inch loaf pan (or deep
baking dish) with olive oil spray. Shape the meat mixture
into a loaf, and place it in the pan. Bake uncovered for about
an hour.

Once the meat loaf is cooked, remove it from the oven,
and let it cool for about 10 minutes. Run a butter knife
along the edges to remove it from the pan, invert it onto a
large serving dish, and slice to serve.

Nutrition Facts (amount per serving)	
Calories	152
Total Fat	7 g
Saturated Fat	2 g
Polyunsaturated Fat	0.2 g
Monounsaturated Fat	0.5 g
Cholesterol	91 mg
Sodium	319 mg
Potassium	68 mg
Total Carbohydrate	4 g
Dietary Fiber	0.6 g
Sugars	0.8 g
Protein	19 g
Calcium 1% • Magnesium 1%	

Italian Herbed Turkey Cutlets

Serves 4

3 small cloves garlic, minced
2 tablespoons chopped fresh rosemary
2 tablespoons chopped fresh parsley
1½ teaspoons chopped fresh sage
½ teaspoon cracked black pepper
4 (4-ounce) boneless, skinless turkey cutlets
Grated zest of 1 large lemon
1 cup low-sodium vegetable broth

Preheat the oven to 375°F.

In a small bowl, mix together the garlic, rosemary, parsley, sage, and pepper. Rub a generous amount of the herb mixture on both sides of each cutlet. Place the turkey cutlets in a 9- by 13-inch baking dish, top with lemon zest, and add the vegetable broth to the dish. Cover with foil, and bake for 20 to 25 minutes. Remove the foil during the last 5 minutes of baking to brown the tops of the cutlets. Remove from the oven and serve immediately.

Nutrition Facts (amount per serving)	
Calories	129
Total Fat	2 g
Saturated Fat	0.6 g
Polyunsaturated Fat	0.3 g
Monounsaturated Fat	0.6 g
Cholesterol	49 mg
Sodium	1188 mg
Potassium	373 mg
Total Carbohydrate	7 g
Dietary Fiber	1 g
Sugars	5 g
Protein	19.6 g
Calcium 3% • Magnesium 6%	

Turkey Roulade with Cider Sauce
Serves 4

5 tablespoons extra virgin olive oil, divided

½ cup diced white onion, divided

4 cremini mushrooms, thinly sliced

2 cups spinach

3 medium cloves garlic, minced

½ cup white wine

1½ cups low-sodium chicken broth, divided

⅓ cup dried cranberries

3 slices 100% whole wheat bread, cut into ½-inch squares

½ cup chopped almonds

1 large fresh sage leaf, finely minced

1 teaspoon chopped fresh thyme

1 teaspoon chopped fresh parsley

1 (2-pound) skinless, boneless turkey breast

¼ teaspoon sea salt

½ teaspoon cracked black pepper

CIDER SAUCE

1½ cups cider, divided

1 tablespoon cornstarch

½–1 cup roasting liquid from turkey

Preheat the oven to 375°F.

To make the filling for the roulade, heat 2 tablespoons of the oil in a large pan over medium heat. Add ¼ cup of the onion along with the mushrooms, spinach, and garlic, and cook until the onion is translucent. Add the white wine, and simmer for about a minute to let the alcohol cook out. Add ½ cup of the broth along with the cranberries. Once the broth is hot (but not boiling), add the bread, almonds, and fresh herbs. Cook for 2 to 3 minutes, and then stir. The filling should not be too soupy.

Butterfly the turkey breast by placing your hand flat on top of the breast and cutting sideways into the breast, making sure not to cut through completely. Open the butterflied breast and place it between two sheets of plastic wrap. Flatten the turkey with a mallet to ½-inch thickness. Season both sides with salt and pepper. Spread the filling on the turkey, keeping it toward the center. Roll up the turkey breast and secure it with kitchen twine at three places (middle and two ends). Bring the pan in which you cooked the filling to high heat, and sear the rolled turkey breast to a brown color on both sides, 3 to 4 minutes per side.

Drizzle the remaining 3 tablespoons of oil in a medium roasting pan. Add the rest of the onion and broth. Place the turkey in the center of the pan, cover with foil, and bake for approximately 1 hour.

To the turkey-searing pan, add ¾ cup of the cider, and scrape the bottom of the pan to mix in the juices. In a small bowl, whisk the rest of the cider with the cornstarch, and add to the pan. Boil for 2 to 3 minutes, until the sauce thickens.

After removing the turkey from the oven, add up to 1 cup of the roasting juices to the cider sauce, and mix well. Keep the turkey covered, and let it sit for 10 minutes. Remove the turkey from the roasting pan, and cut off the twine. Slice the turkey, and top each slice with cider sauce.

Nutrition Facts (amount per serving)	
Calories	518
Total Fat	14 g
Saturated Fat	2 g
Polyunsaturated Fat	3 g
Monounsaturated Fat	9 g
Cholesterol	80 mg
Sodium	2,788 mg
Potassium	314 mg
Total Carbohydrate	44 g
Dietary Fiber	4 g
Sugars	9 g
Protein	50 g
Calcium 8% • Magnesium 16%	

Stuffed Bell Peppers
Serves 4

2 tablespoons extra virgin olive oil

½ small white onion, chopped

2 small cloves garlic, minced

½ cup chopped carrot

¼ teaspoon dried thyme

¼ teaspoon dried basil

½ pound 95%-lean ground beef

1 cup chopped zucchini

1 tablespoon chopped fresh parsley

1 (15-ounce) can kidney beans, rinsed and drained

4 large red bell peppers

2 cups low-sodium marinara sauce

Preheat the oven to 350°F.

Heat the oil in a large pan over medium to high heat. Add the onion, garlic, carrot, thyme, and basil. Cook for 1 to 2 minutes, and then add the beef, breaking up any clumps with a spatula. Once the beef starts to brown, after about 5 to 6 minutes, add the zucchini, parsley, and kidney beans. Cook for 5 more minutes, or until the beef is no longer pink.

To prepare the peppers, cut the tops off just below the stems. Remove the seeds and ribs. Fill each pepper with the meat mixture, and place in an 8-inch square baking dish so that the peppers are standing upright. Pour water into the dish to cover the bottom. Cover the pan with foil, and bake for 20 to 25 minutes, or until the peppers are tender when pierced with a fork.

Heat the marinara sauce in a small saucepan, and pour over each plated bell pepper before serving.

Nutrition Facts (amount per serving)	
Calories	443
Total Fat	22 g
Saturated Fat	6 g
Polyunsaturated Fat	2 g
Monounsaturated Fat	10 g
Cholesterol	43 mg
Sodium	988 mg
Potassium	937 mg
Total Carbohydrate	46 g
Dietary Fiber	12 g
Sugars	13 g
Protein	20 g
Calcium 11% • Magnesium 18%	

Sesame Salmon Fillets

Serves 2

1 tablespoon sesame oil
2 (4-ounce) salmon fillets, skin on
⅛ teaspoon ground ginger
⅛ teaspoon sea salt
⅛ teaspoon cracked black pepper
2 teaspoons black sesame seeds

Heat the oil in a medium pan over medium heat. Once the pan is hot, add the salmon, skin side down. Top each fillet with the ginger powder, salt, pepper, and sesame seeds. Pat the seeds down softly so they stick to the fillet. After about 3 to 4 minutes, turn the fillets over, and sear the other side. After 1 to 2 minutes, remove the fillets from the pan and serve immediately.

Serving Suggestion: Serve with sautéed greens or broccoli and whole wheat couscous.

Nutrition Facts (amount per serving)	
Calories	319
Total Fat	21 g
Saturated Fat	3 g
Polyunsaturated Fat	9 g
Monounsaturated Fat	7 g
Cholesterol	81 mg
Sodium	204 mg
Potassium	756 mg
Total Carbohydrate	2 g
Dietary Fiber	1 g
Sugars	0.1 g
Protein	31 g
Calcium 11% • Magnesium 18%	

Spice-Rubbed Salmon
Serves 4

2 teaspoons chili powder

1 teaspoon ground cumin

1 teaspoon brown sugar

⅛ teaspoon sea salt

⅛ teaspoon cracked black pepper

4 (4-ounce) salmon fillets

Juice of ½ orange

2 tablespoons extra virgin olive oil

In a small bowl, mix the chili powder, cumin, sugar, salt, and pepper. Rub the mixture onto each salmon fillet by hand.

Heat the oil in a nonstick pan over medium heat. Once the oil is hot, add two fillets, skin side down, to the pan at a time, and cook for 1 to 2 minutes. Then turn the fillets over, and squeeze orange juice over them. Cook for another 1 to 2 minutes, until the fillets are flaky and can be separated with a fork. Repeat the process with the second set of fillets. Serve immediately.

Nutrition Facts (amount per serving)	
Calories	295
Total Fat	18 g
Saturated Fat	3 g
Polyunsaturated Fat	5 g
Monounsaturated Fat	9 g
Cholesterol	81 mg
Sodium	78 mg
Potassium	776 mg
Total Carbohydrate	3 g
Dietary Fiber	0.9 g
Sugars	2 g
Protein	29 g
Calcium 3% • Magnesium 12%	

Pan-Steamed Orange Roughy
Serves 4

4 small green onions, white ends cut off

4 teaspoons chopped fresh ginger

4 (3-ounce) orange roughy fillets

3 large cloves garlic, minced

¼ teaspoon cracked black pepper

½ teaspoon black sesame seeds

1 lime, very thinly sliced

2 teaspoons sesame oil

Cut four sheets of foil, about 6 by 6 inches. In the center of each sheet, place a green onion, along with 1 teaspoon of ginger. Place one fillet on top, and sprinkle with garlic, pepper, and sesame seeds. Place four paper-thin slices of lime on top of each fillet, and drizzle with sesame oil. Wrap each fillet by folding the foil up from the sides, meeting in the middle and folding down to seal.

Heat a large flat pan over medium-high heat, and place the foil-wrapped fillets in the pan. Cook for 8 to 10 minutes. Remove the fish packages from the pan, and let sit 3 to 4 minutes to continue steaming in the foil. Serve in the foil, so that each person can unwrap his or her dinner.

Nutrition Facts *(amount per serving)*	
Calories	120
Total Fat	4 g
Saturated Fat	0.4 g
Polyunsaturated Fat	1 g
Monounsaturated Fat	2 g
Cholesterol	22 mg
Sodium	74 mg
Potassium	438 mg
Total Carbohydrate	5 g
Dietary Fiber	1 g
Sugars	1 g
Protein	17 g
Calcium 7% • Magnesium 11%	

Fish Tacos
Serves 4

4 (3-ounce) mahi mahi fillets
3 tablespoons extra virgin olive oil
4 cups thinly shredded red cabbage
3 tablespoons red wine vinegar
8 corn tortillas
½ teaspoon ground cumin
⅛ teaspoon cracked black pepper
2 large avocados, pitted, peeled, and thinly sliced
3 large Roma tomatoes, chopped

SAUCE
¾ cup low-fat plain Greek yogurt
¼ cup low-fat milk
Juice of 1 large lemon
⅛ teaspoon cracked black pepper
⅛ teaspoon sea salt

To make the sauce, whisk all ingredients together in a small bowl. The consistency of the sauce should be relatively thin, to drizzle over the top of the tacos, adding more milk if it isn't thin enough. Set aside.

Heat a large pan over medium heat. Season both sides of each fillet with cumin and pepper. Add the oil to the hot pan, and when the oil is hot add the fillets, two at a time. Cook each side about 3 to 4 minutes, or until each side is seared and the center of the fish is no longer transparent. Remove from the pan, and drain on paper towels. Repeat with the other two fillets.

In a separate bowl, toss the cabbage with the vinegar. With two forks, break apart each fillet into two pieces. Warm the tortillas in a flat pan on low heat, then place a couple of pieces of fish in each tortilla, top with the cabbage mixture, avocado, and chopped tomato, and then drizzle with sauce. Fold tortilla over and serve.

RECIPE TIP

• Substitute any dense fish, including salmon, for the mahi mahi.

Nutrition Facts *(amount per serving)*	
Calories	583
Total Fat	29 g
Saturated Fat	4 g
Polyunsaturated Fat	4 g
Monounsaturated Fat	17 g
Cholesterol	137 mg
Sodium	323 mg
Potassium	1,145 mg
Total Carbohydrate	48 g
Dietary Fiber	14 g
Sugars	6 g
Protein	43 g
Calcium 22% • Magnesium 26%	

Thai Curried Vegetables

Serves 4

2 tablespoons coconut oil

1 medium onion, cut into ¼-inch pieces

1 medium red bell pepper, coarsely chopped

1 medium green bell pepper, coarsely chopped

1 cup coarsely chopped broccoli

3–4 cups cubed eggplant, ½-inch pieces

1 small jalapeño chile pepper, thinly sliced (seeded for less heat)

1 tablespoon chopped fresh ginger

2 large cloves garlic, coarsely chopped

1 teaspoon curry powder

½ teaspoon ground cinnamon

½ teaspoon ground turmeric

½ teaspoon cracked black pepper

2 cups unsweetened light coconut milk

½ cup low-sodium vegetable broth

1 heaping tablespoon unsalted peanut butter

4 tablespoons coarsely chopped Thai basil

Heat a large pot over medium heat, and add the coconut oil. Once it has melted, add the onion, bell peppers, and broccoli, stirring constantly. Add the eggplant, chile pepper, ginger, garlic, curry powder, cinnamon, turmeric, and pepper. Stir to incorporate the ingredients and spices and cook until the eggplant browns and the vegetables soften a bit, about 4 to 5 minutes. Add the coconut milk, broth, and peanut butter. Stir well to incorporate the peanut butter, and then cover the pot. Simmer on low for about 10 minutes. Then remove the lid, and simmer uncovered for an additional 5 minutes, or until the sauce thickens to the desired consistency. Stir in the basil right before serving.

Serving Suggestion: Scoop ½ cup of cooked brown rice into individual bowls, and top each with a large ladleful of veggies and sauce.

Fun Fact: Thai basil has a sharper flavor than Italian basil, with a licorice undertone.

Nutrition Facts *(amount per serving)*	
Calories	270
Total Fat	21 g
Saturated Fat	18 g
Polyunsaturated Fat	0.4 g
Monounsaturated Fat	0.5 g
Cholesterol	0 mg
Sodium	107 mg
Potassium	441 mg
Total Carbohydrate	16 g
Dietary Fiber	5 g
Sugars	2 g
Protein	6 g
Calcium 8% • Magnesium 8%	

Veggie Fajitas
Serves 4

3 large red bell peppers, cut into strips

3 large green bell peppers, cut into strips

3 large yellow bell peppers, cut into strips

2 large green zucchini, cut into strips

2 large portobello mushrooms about 6 inches in diameter

2 large white onions, sliced

3 tablespoons extra virgin olive oil

3 cloves garlic, minced

1½ teaspoons dried oregano

¼ teaspoon ground cumin

⅛ teaspoon cracked black pepper

⅛ teaspoon sea salt

8 corn tortillas

Cut the bell peppers into ½-inch strips. Cut the zucchini lengthwise into thin strips, and then cut each strip in half. Wipe the mushrooms with a damp towel, snap the stems off, scoop the gills out with a metal tablespoon, and cut into ½-inch strips. Cut the onions into ½-inch slices.

Heat the oil in a large pot over medium-high heat. Once the oil is hot, add the bell peppers, zucchini, mushrooms, onions, garlic, oregano, cumin, pepper, and salt. Cook until the veggies are soft and the onions translucent, about 5 to 6 minutes.

Warm the tortillas in a flat pan over medium heat, spoon in the veggies. Fold the tortilla over and serve.

Serving Suggestion: Serve with black beans and be creative with toppings, such as plain Greek yogurt (in place of sour cream), salsa, shredded lettuce, guacamole, or low-fat shredded cheese.

Nutrition Facts (amount per serving)	
Calories	343
Total Fat	13 g
Saturated Fat	2 g
Polyunsaturated Fat	8 g
Monounsaturated Fat	8 g
Cholesterol	0 mg
Sodium	89 mg
Potassium	795 mg
Total Carbohydrate	55 g
Dietary Fiber	14 g
Sugars	7 g
Protein	12 g
Calcium 17% • Magnesium 21%	

Grilled Portobello Burger with Caramelized Onions and Pesto

Serves 4

4 medium portobello mushrooms (about 4 inches in diameter)

4 tablespoons extra virgin olive oil

¼ teaspoon sea salt

½ teaspoon ground black pepper

8 tablespoons balsamic vinegar

4 100% whole wheat hamburger buns

4 tablespoons prepared pesto

4 tablespoons Caramelized Onions (see page 155)

Clean the mushrooms by wiping them with a damp towel. Remove the mushroom stems, and then scoop out the brown gills with a metal spoon and discard them. Brush each mushroom top with a tablespoon of oil, and sprinkle the inside of each mushroom with salt, pepper, and 2 tablespoons of balsamic vinegar. Set aside for at least 20 minutes.

Place the mushrooms on a hot grill or grill pan, top down. Grill for about 5 to 7 minutes, and then flip and grill for another 5 or 7 minutes, or until tender. Don't handle them too much to prevent the juices from being released.

Toast the buns while the mushrooms are grilling by placing them face down on the grill for about 1 minute. Remove from the grill, and spread 1 tablespoon of pesto on the inside of each top bun. Place a mushroom on each bottom bun, then top with 1 tablespoon of caramelized onions.

RECIPE TIP
• Add romaine lettuce, tomato, or any other sliced vegetables of your choice for more vitamins and minerals.

Nutrition Facts (amount per serving)	
Calories	424
Total Fat	25 g
Saturated Fat	4 g
Polyunsaturated Fat	3 g
Monounsaturated Fat	10 g
Cholesterol	0 mg
Sodium	607 mg
Potassium	40 mg
Total Carbohydrate	45 g
Dietary Fiber	6 g
Sugars	6 g
Protein	10 g
Calcium 10% • Magnesium 1%	

Caramelized Onions

Makes 10 (2-tablespoon) servings

2 tablespoons extra virgin olive oil

4 cups, thinly sliced white onions

1 teaspoon brown sugar

⅛ teaspoon cracked black pepper

Heat a medium-sized saucepan over medium heat. Add the oil and when the oil is hot, add the onions, and then the sugar and pepper. Sauté for 5 to 10 minutes, stirring constantly to avoid burning. Once the onions are translucent and start turning brown, cover the pan and turn the heat down to low. Let the onions "sweat" for about 5 more minutes. When done, they should be dark brown and very soft.

Nutrition Facts *(amount per serving)*	
Calories	43
Total Fat	3 g
Saturated Fat	.04 g
Polyunsaturated Fat	.04 g
Monounsaturated Fat	2 g
Cholesterol	0 mg
Sodium	2 mg
Potassium	74 mg
Total Carbohydrate	5 g
Dietary Fiber	.08 g
Sugars	.06 g
Protein	.05 g
Calcium 1% • Magnesium 1%	

Mediterranean Bowl
Serves 4

1 cup uncooked whole wheat couscous

1¼ cups water

1 (16-ounce) can artichoke hearts

½ cup rinsed, drained, and pitted kalamata olives

1 (12-ounce) jar roasted red peppers, rinsed, drained and
coarsely chopped

½ cup low-fat feta cheese

1 cup chopped cherry tomatoes

½ small red onion, finely diced

¼ teaspoon finely chopped fresh oregano

¼ teaspoon finely chopped fresh mint

Pinch of chile pepper flakes

4 tablespoons extra virgin olive oil

Juice of 1 lemon

Cracked black pepper

Boil the water, add the couscous, stir, and turn the heat off. Cover the pot with a lid and let sit for 5 minutes, and fluff with a fork prior to serving.

Combine all ingredients, except the cooked couscous, and mix thoroughly. Refrigerate for 15 to 20 minutes, and then fold in the couscous. Serve cold, or at room temperature.

Serving Suggestion: Great alongside salmon fillets or chicken breast, or mixed into chicken or tuna salad.

HEALTH TIP
• Many jarred olives come in a brining liquid packed with salt. Just rinse and drain the olives to remove much of the salt.

Nutrition Facts *(amount per serving)*	
Calories	433
Total Fat	20 g
Saturated Fat	5 g
Polyunsaturated Fat	3 g
Monounsaturated Fat	12 g
Cholesterol	17 mg
Sodium	432 mg
Potassium	513 mg
Total Carbohydrate	54 g
Dietary Fiber	12 g
Sugars	0 g
Protein	13 g
Calcium 15% • Magnesium 12%	

Grilled Veggie Pizza
Serves 6

2 medium portobello mushrooms about 4 inches in diameter
1 small yellow zucchini, cut in half lengthwise
1 small red onion, cut into rounds
4 tablespoons extra-virgin olive oil
⅛ teaspoon salt
⅛ teaspoon cracked black pepper
1 (1-pound) whole wheat pizza dough
2 plum tomatoes, thinly sliced
½ cup shredded skim mozzarella cheese
¼ cup fresh basil leaves, coarsely chopped

Preheat the oven to 400°F.

Heat a grill or grill pan over medium heat. Wipe the mushrooms with a damp towel, snap the stems off, scoop the gills out with a metal tablespoon, and cut into ½-inch strips. Brush the mushrooms, zucchini, and onion with 2 tablespoons of the oil, and sprinkle on salt and pepper. Place the veggies on the grill, and cook covered for about 6 minutes, turning once, until tender and browned. Remove from the grill, and separate the onion rings.

Coat a cookie sheet with olive oil spray. Stretch the pizza dough with your hands onto the cookie sheet, or roll out the dough on a floured surface to prevent sticking. Pierce the dough with a fork in several spots so it does not fluff up when it bakes. Drizzle the dough with the remaining 2 tablespoons olive oil, spreading with your fingers or a spatula, and bake 12 to 15 minutes, or until crispy.

Remove the pizza crust from the oven, and quickly top with the veggies and cheese. Return to the oven just until the cheese melts, 5 to 6 minutes.

Remove from the oven, top with basil, and serve.

RECIPE ALTERATIONS
• Top the dough with low-sodium marinara sauce before baking for a different flavor.
• Switch up the vegetables or add more veggies.
• Cut the dough in half if you prefer thin crust pizza.
• Precooked pizza crust works well, too. Just look for 100% whole wheat crust.

Nutrition Facts (amount per serving)	
Calories	159
Total Fat	6 g
Saturated Fat	2 g
Polyunsaturated Fat	0.5 g
Monounsaturated Fat	3 g
Cholesterol	11 mg
Sodium	299 mg
Potassium	112 mg
Total Carbohydrate	18 g
Dietary Fiber	3 g
Sugars	0.5 g
Protein	8 g
Calcium 17% • Magnesium 3%	

Mexican Pizza

Serves 6

½ cup rinsed and drained canned black beans

1 tablespoon canned chipotle pepper sauce

3 tablespoons water

1 (12-inch) prebaked 100% whole wheat thin-crust pizza

1 small zucchini, thinly sliced in rounds

½ cup thinly sliced red onion

½ cup sliced red bell pepper

½ cup shredded skim mozzarella cheese

½ teaspoon dried oregano

Preheat the oven to 400°F. In a blender or food processor, combine the black beans, chipotle sauce, and water. Puree until smooth. Evenly spread the mixture on the pizza crust. Cover with zucchini rounds, then bell peppers and onions, and finally cheese. Sprinkle oregano on top, and bake for about 15 minutes, or until the cheese is bubbling and browning.

RECIPE ALTERATION

• This pizza can also be prepared with 100% whole wheat pizza dough, as described in the Grilled Veggie Pizza recipe (page 158).

Nutrition Facts *(amount per serving)*	
Calories	18
Total Fat	7 g
Saturated Fat	6 g
Polyunsaturated Fat	2 g
Monounsaturated Fat	10 g
Cholesterol	11 mg
Sodium	303 mg
Potassium	122 mg
Total Carbohydrate	21 g
Dietary Fiber	4 g
Sugars	0.3 g
Protein	9 g
Calcium 14% • Magnesium 5%	

Healthier Mac 'n' Cheese

Serves 4

½ cup water

1 large white onion, sliced

8 medium cloves garlic, halved

⅛ teaspoon sea salt

⅛ teaspoon cracked black pepper

1 teaspoon brown mustard

8 ounces 100% whole wheat macaroni pasta

1 cup coarsely chopped broccoli florets

Pinch of chile pepper flakes

⅓ cup low-fat ricotta cheese, divided

1 cup shredded low-fat cheddar cheese, divided

½ cup whole wheat bread crumbs*

½ cup grated Parmesan cheese

¼ teaspoon dried basil

1 tablespoon chopped fresh parsley

Whole wheat bread crumbs: Place toasted or stale whole wheat bread slices into a food processor, and pulse until coarse crumbs form.

Preheat the oven to 425°F. Coat a 9- by 9-inch baking dish with olive oil spray, and set aside.

In a medium saucepan, add the water, onion, and garlic. Cover with a lid and simmer over low heat for about 10 minutes, or until onion and garlic can easily be mashed with a fork. Put the mixture into a blender, add salt, pepper, and mustard, and pulse to combine.

Bring a large pot of water to boil. Add the pasta, and cook according to package directions, until al dente. In the last few minutes of boiling the pasta, add the broccoli, and cover the pot. After about 3 minutes, drain the pasta and broccoli, and run under cold water so that the pasta does not keep cooking.

Heat the pasta pot over low heat, and add the onion-garlic paste, chile pepper flakes, and 2 tablespoons of the ricotta. Stir until the cheese is incorporated, and then slowly stir in the rest of the ricotta with a whisk. Add half of the cheddar cheese, and stir until melted. Then add the rest of the cheddar cheese, and stir until melted. Add the cooked pasta and broccoli, and stir with a large spoon until the sauce covers most of the pasta. Transfer to the baking dish, and top with the bread crumbs, Parmesan cheese, and basil. Bake for about 10 minutes, or until the bread crumbs and Parmesan start to brown. Remove from the oven, top with parsley, and serve warm.

RECIPE ALTERATIONS

- If you do not have macaroni, substitute with whole wheat rotini pasta or whole wheat penne pasta.
- Use just about any veggies, such as cauliflower, zucchini, bell peppers, and spinach.
- Low-fat cottage cheese can be used in place of ricotta cheese. Add it to the onion-garlic mixture in the blender, to avoid lumpy mac 'n' cheese.

Nutrition Facts *(amount per serving)*	
Calories	366
Total Fat	9 g
Saturated Fat	5 g
Polyunsaturated Fat	0.3 g
Monounsaturated Fat	2 g
Cholesterol	22 mg
Sodium	511 mg
Potassium	218 mg
Total Carbohydrate	44 g
Dietary Fiber	8 g
Sugars	0.7 g
Protein	25 g
Calcium 29% • Magnesium 7%	

Anna's Black Beans

Serves 8

4 cups dried black beans

1–2 bay leaves

¾ teaspoon ground cumin

3 teaspoons sea salt

¼ small white onion, slivered

2–3 large cloves garlic, whole

1–2 dried red chiles/chiles de arbol

8–10 cups water

Place all the ingredients in a large pot, and bring to a boil. Lower the heat, and simmer for 2 to 3 hours. Check and stir every 30 to 40 minutes, adding water if necessary.

TIPS

• These beans can be served as a side dish to your breakfast, lunch, or dinner with or without the broth.

• Enjoy the beans and broth as a soup. The broth contains minerals and vitamins released from the beans as they cooked.

• Soaking the beans overnight in water reduces cooking time in half. It also means less cooking water, because the beans won't absorb as much.

• This recipe can be scaled: for every cup of dried beans, use 3 to 4 cups water.

• Black beans can be replaced by just about any other bean: kidney, pinto, navy, white.

Nutrition Facts (amount per serving)	
Calories	119
Total Fat	0.5 g
Saturated Fat	0.1 g
Polyunsaturated Fat	0.2 g
Monounsaturated Fat	0.1 g
Cholesterol	0 mg
Sodium	912 mg
Potassium	320 mg
Total Carbohydrate	21 g
Dietary Fiber	8 g
Sugars	0 g
Protein	8 g
Calcium 3% • Magnesium 16%	

Pinto Beans
Serves 8

2 cups dried pinto beans

1 bay leaf

2 large cloves garlic, whole

1 large jalapeño chile pepper, top cut off

4–5 slivers white onion

1 tablespoon sea salt

6 cups water

Place all the ingredients in a large pot, and bring to a boil. Lower the heat, and simmer for 2 to 3 hours. Check and stir every 30 to 40 minutes, adding water if necessary.

TIPS

• These beans can be served as a side dish to your breakfast, lunch, or dinner with or without the broth.

• For mashed beans, strain the beans and mash them with a potato masher, adding some broth to smooth them out.

• Enjoy the beans and broth as a soup. The broth contains minerals and vitamins released from the beans as they cooked.

• Soaking the beans overnight in water reduces cooking time in half. It also means less cooking water, because the beans won't absorb as much.

• This recipe can be scaled: For every cup of dried beans, use 3 to 4 cups water.

Nutrition Facts *(amount per serving)*	
Calories	63
Total Fat	0.3 g
Saturated Fat	0.1 g
Polyunsaturated Fat	0 g
Monounsaturated Fat	0 g
Cholesterol	0 mg
Sodium	543 mg
Potassium	216 mg
Total Carbohydrate	12 g
Dietary Fiber	4 g
Sugars	0.1 g
Protein	4 g
Calcium 3% • Magnesium 7%	

Pumpkin Soup with Whole Wheat Parmesan Croutons

Serves 6

CROUTONS

2 slices 100% whole wheat bread

4 tablespoons extra virgin olive oil

3 tablespoons grated Parmesan cheese

1 teaspoon dried Italian herbs (premixed, or use thyme, rosemary, oregano, parsley, and basil)

⅛ teaspoon cracked black pepper

SOUP

2 tablespoons extra virgin olive oil

½ small onion, chopped

1 cup diced carrot

3 small cloves garlic, minced

2 cups canned pumpkin puree

⅛ teaspoon ground ginger

⅛ teaspoon ground cinnamon

1½ teaspoons dried parsley

Pinch of chile pepper flakes

1½ liters low-sodium vegetable or chicken broth

Preheat the oven to 400°F. To make the croutons, toast the whole wheat bread, cut the slices into small cubes, and place on a cookie sheet. Drizzle with oil, and sprinkle with Parmesan, herbs, and pepper. Bake in the oven for about 5 minutes, or until crispy.

For the soup, heat the oil in a large pot over medium heat. Add the onion, carrot, and garlic. Cook for 4 to 5 minutes, until the onion browns and becomes translucent. Add the pumpkin, ginger, cinnamon, parsley, and chile pepper flakes, and sauté for about 1 minute. Add the broth, and bring to a boil. Lower the heat, and simmer for about 10 minutes. Ladle into bowls to serve, and top with two or three croutons per bowl.

Nutrition Facts (amount per serving)	
Calories	190
Total Fat	11 g
Saturated Fat	2 g
Polyunsaturated Fat	2 g
Monounsaturated Fat	7 g
Cholesterol	2 mg
Sodium	609 mg
Potassium	290 mg
Total Carbohydrate	20 g
Dietary Fiber	5 g
Sugars	8 g
Protein	4 g
Calcium 10% • Magnesium 7%	

Cauliflower Carrot Soup

Serves 6

1 large head cauliflower, coarsely chopped (about 8 cups)

2 tablespoons extra virgin olive oil

½ small white onion, chopped

2 large cloves garlic, chopped

1 cup chopped carrot

1 quart low-sodium vegetable broth

½ teaspoon sea salt

½ teaspoon cracked black pepper

⅛ teaspoon chile pepper flakes

⅛ teaspoon dried basil

Fill a large pot with water, and bring it to a boil. Remove the outer leaves of the cauliflower head, and then cut out the core. Coarsely chop the cauliflower, and add it to the boiling water. Cover the pot, and boil for 6 or 8 minutes, or until a fork easily pierces the cauliflower pieces. Strain the cauliflower, and discard the water.

Heat the oil in the same pot over medium heat. Add the onion, garlic, and carrot, and sauté until the onion is translucent. Add the cauliflower. Transfer a ladleful of veggies to a blender. Add 1 cup of broth, and blend on low to combine, then on high until smooth. Transfer the blended veggies to another large pot, and repeat the process until all the veggies are blended.

Heat the blended veggies over medium-high heat, and season with salt, pepper, chile pepper flakes, and basil. Bring to a boil, and serve hot.

Nutrition Facts (amount per serving)	
Calories	109
Total Fat	5 g
Saturated Fat	0.7 g
Polyunsaturated Fat	0.8 g
Monounsaturated Fat	3 g
Cholesterol	0 mg
Sodium	409 mg
Potassium	498 mg
Total Carbohydrate	14 g
Dietary Fiber	5 g
Sugars	3 g
Protein	4 g
Calcium 5% • Magnesium 6%	

Roasted Butternut Squash Soup
Serves 6

1 large butternut squash or 2 (16-ounce) bags precut butternut
squash (to skip the roasting)

2 tablespoons extra virgin olive oil

1 large clove garlic

½ white onion, chopped

2½ liters low-sodium vegetable or chicken broth, divided

⅛ teaspoon cracked black pepper

¼ teaspoon white pepper

1 tablespoon chopped fresh parsley

¼ teaspoon chile pepper flakes

1 teaspoon finely chopped fresh rosemary

3–4 finely minced fresh sage leaves

The squash can be roasted a day or two ahead. Just store
the roasted squash in an airtight container in the refrigerator.

Preheat the oven to 400°F. Cut off the top of the squash,
and then cut the squash in half lengthwise, and scoop out
the seeds from the center with a metal spoon until there are
no strings or seeds left. Coat a cookie sheet with olive oil
spray, and place the squash on it, cut sides down. Roast in
the oven for about 30 minutes, or until the squash is soft to
the touch. Remove from the oven, and let cool completely.

In a large pot over medium heat, add the oil, garlic, and
onion. Sauté a few minutes, until the onion turns light
brown. While the onion and garlic are cooking, scoop out
the roasted squash from its skin with a spoon, and add to
the pot. Mix together, using a spatula to break up large
chunks of squash. Add 1 liter of broth, and bring to a boil.
Reduce the heat to low, and transfer the veggies in batches
to a blender, leaving most of the liquid in the pot. Blend the

squash on low to mix, and then on high until smooth. If the squash won't blend easily, add a bit of the broth. Once all the squash has been blended, return it to the pot, add the rest of the broth as well as the black pepper, white pepper, parsley, chili pepper flakes, rosemary and sage. Bring the soup to a boil and serve hot.

Serving Suggestion: Swirl a teaspoon of low-fat sour cream or yogurt into each bowl of soup, and then sprinkle fresh parsley on top before serving.

COOKING TIP

• If using precut squash, just sauté over medium heat with extra virgin olive oil until tender.

Nutrition Facts *(amount per serving)*	
Calories	158
Total Fat	6 g
Saturated Fat	0.9 g
Polyunsaturated Fat	0.9 g
Monounsaturated Fat	4 g
Cholesterol	0 mg
Sodium	699 mg
Potassium	425 mg
Total Carbohydrate	24 g
Dietary Fiber	6 g
Sugars	5 g
Protein	3 g
Calcium 10% • Magnesium 11%	

Broccoli Soup
Serves 4

8 cups coarsely chopped broccoli

2 tablespoons extra virgin olive oil

1 cup chopped white onion

2 large cloves garlic

3 cups low-sodium chicken broth

⅛ teaspoon chile pepper flakes

¼ teaspoon cracked black pepper

½ cup low-fat milk

Bring a large pot of water to a boil. Add the broccoli, and boil about 8 to 10 minutes, or until an inserted fork easily pierces the stems. Drain the broccoli, and set aside. In the same pot, heat the oil over medium heat. Add the onion and garlic, and cook for about 2 minutes, stirring until the onion is translucent. Add the cooked broccoli and the broth to the pot, and simmer for another 4 to 5 minutes. Turn off the heat, and transfer the veggies and a little bit of broth in small batches to a blender. Blend on low at first, and then on high until smooth. Pour the blended soup into another pot, and repeat until all of the broccoli mixture has been blended. Add chile pepper flakes, black pepper, and milk to the soup, and bring to a boil. Ladle into bowls and serve.

Serving Suggestion: Top with shredded cheddar cheese or whole wheat croutons before serving.

Nutrition Facts *(amount per serving)*	
Calories	291
Total Fat	14 g
Saturated Fat	5 g
Polyunsaturated Fat	2 g
Monounsaturated Fat	7 g
Cholesterol	24 mg
Sodium	227 mg
Potassium	641 mg
Total Carbohydrate	28 g
Dietary Fiber	6 g
Sugars	14 g
Protein	17 g
Calcium 45% • Magnesium 12%	

Mom's Bean Soup
Serves 4

6 cups pinto beans in broth (see Pinto Beans, page 166)

¼ cup chopped white onion

½ cup chopped Roma tomato

2 large avocados, peeled, pitted, and cubed

4 tablespoons chopped fresh cilantro

4 tablespoons shredded low-fat Monterey Jack cheese

4 teaspoons canned chipotle pepper sauce

Bring the beans to a boil in a medium pot over medium to high heat. Turn the heat off. Ladle 1½ cups of the beans with broth into four bowls. Top each bowl with the raw, chopped onion, tomato, avocado, cilantro, shredded cheese, and chipotle sauce. Serve immediately.

Personal Note from Chef Anna: This is a very nostalgic dish for me. Growing up, we often had this soup for dinner. One large pot of beans would feed my sisters and me for the week and we would never get tired of them. We also loved helping our mom chop all the ingredients and shred the cheese.

Nutrition Facts (amount per serving)	
Calories	258
Total Fat	19 g
Saturated Fat	3 g
Polyunsaturated Fat	2 g
Monounsaturated Fat	9 g
Cholesterol	2 mg
Sodium	620 mg
Potassium	774 mg
Total Carbohydrate	25 g
Dietary Fiber	11 g
Sugars	0.4 g
Protein	8 g
Calcium 10% • Magnesium 16%	

Appetizers and Side Dishes

Completing a meal with appetizers and side dishes can sometimes be a challenge. Store-bought or premade options are very convenient, but are also loaded with heavy ingredients such as full-fat cream cheese, mayonnaise, sour cream, and butter and can be very high in sodium. Frozen appetizers and side dishes are also abundant and easy to throw into the oven, but why not offer your guests or family something fresh, healthy, and delicious that won't weigh them down? Here you will find traditional appetizers and sides with a healthy twist as well as new ideas to try for your next party.

Black Bean and Apple Salsa

Serves 6 (Makes 3 cups)

1 (15-ounce) can black beans, rinsed and drained

½ large Granny Smith apple, cubed

¼ cup finely chopped red onion

½ medium serrano chile pepper, unseeded and finely chopped

3 tablespoons chopped fresh cilantro

Juice of ½ large lime

Juice of ½ large orange

⅛ teaspoon cracked black pepper

⅛ teaspoon sea salt

Combine all the ingredients in a large bowl. Before serving, refrigerate for at least 20 minutes so that the flavors blend.

Serving Suggestion: Serve atop a chicken breast, or as a snack or appetizer with unsalted, baked tortilla chips.

VARIATION

• To make this salsa less spicy, remove the seeds from the serrano chile pepper by slicing it into fourths lengthwise and cutting out the ribs and seeds.

Nutrition Facts (amount per serving)	
Calories	100
Total Fat	0.4 g
Saturated Fat	0.1 g
Polyunsaturated Fat	0.2 g
Monounsaturated Fat	0 g
Cholesterol	0 mg
Sodium	50 g
Potassium	281 mg
Total Carbohydrate	20 g
Dietary Fiber	6 g
Sugars	3 g
Protein	5 g
Calcium 3% • Magnesium 11%	

Tropical Salsa

Serves 10 (Makes 5 cups)

1 large mango, peeled, pitted, and diced

2 large avocados, peeled, pitted, and diced

1 small red bell pepper, diced

2 large Roma tomatoes, diced

½ cup diced red onion

3 tablespoons chopped fresh cilantro

½ large jalapeño chile pepper, finely chopped (seeded for less heat)

Juice of 1 lime

⅛ teaspoon sea salt

⅛ teaspoon cracked black pepper

Combine all the ingredients in a large bowl. Before serving, refrigerate for at least 20 minutes so that the flavors blend.

Nutrition Facts (amount per serving)	
Calories	82
Total Fat	6 g
Saturated Fat	0.8 g
Polyunsaturated Fat	0.7 g
Monounsaturated Fat	3 g
Cholesterol	0 mg
Sodium	35 mg
Potassium	306 mg
Total Carbohydrate	9 g
Dietary Fiber	3 g
Sugars	3 g
Protein	1 g
Calcium 1% • Magnesium 4%	

Grandma's Guacamole
Serves 8 (Makes about 4 cups)

6 large avocados, pitted

½ cup chopped Roma tomato

¼ cup chopped white onion

¼ cup chopped fresh cilantro

Juice of 3–4 limes

½ teaspoon sea salt

½ teaspoon cracked black pepper

2 tablespoons extra virgin olive oil

½ jalapeño or serrano chile pepper, finely chopped, optional

When pitting the avocados, reserve two pits for later use. Scoop the flesh out, and put it in a large bowl. Mash with a fork or potato masher to the desired consistency. Add the remaining ingredients, and mix well. Store the guacamole with the two pits to help slow the oxidation, or browning, process.

Nutrition Facts (amount per serving)	
Calories	258
Total Fat	24 g
Saturated Fat	3 g
Polyunsaturated Fat	3 g
Monounsaturated Fat	15 g
Cholesterol	0 mg
Sodium	157 mg
Potassium	720 mg
Total Carbohydrate	14 g
Dietary Fiber	9 g
Sugars	0.7 g
Protein	3 g
Calcium 2% • Magnesium 10%	

Chipotle Dip

Serves 4 (Makes 1 cup)

1 tablespoon extra virgin olive oil

½ small white onion, chopped

2 large cloves garlic, minced

2 teaspoons canned chipotle pepper sauce

1 cup low-fat plain Greek yogurt

⅛ teaspoon sea salt

⅛ teaspoon cracked black pepper

Heat the oil in a small pan over medium-high heat. Once hot, add the onion and garlic, and cook for a few minutes, until the onion is translucent. Add the chipotle sauce, and mix it in with the onion and garlic. Remove the pan from the heat. Transfer the mixture to another bowl, and add the yogurt. Mix well, season with salt and pepper to taste. Refrigerate for 20 to 30 minutes before serving.

Serving Suggestion: Serve as a dip with corn chips or fresh vegetables, or as a sauce for fajitas or wraps.

Nutrition Facts *(amount per serving)*	
Calories	78
Total Fat	5 g
Saturated Fat	1 g
Polyunsaturated Fat	0.5 g
Monounsaturated Fat	3 g
Cholesterol	4 mg
Sodium	98 g
Potassium	177 mg
Total Carbohydrate	7 g
Dietary Fiber	0.4 g
Sugars	4 g
Protein	4 g
Calcium 12% • Magnesium 3%	

French Onion Dip

Serves 8 (Makes 2 cups)

2 tablespoons extra virgin olive oil
1 small white onion, chopped
2 cloves garlic, minced
1 cup low-fat plain Greek yogurt
1 cup low-fat sour cream
2 tablespoons Worcestershire sauce
⅛ teaspoon sea salt
⅛ teaspoon cracked black pepper
Minced chives, for garnish

Heat the oil in a small pan over low heat. Add the onion and garlic, and sauté until the onion becomes brown and tender. (Keep the heat low, and move the onion minimally to "sweat" it.) Remove from heat.

In a separate bowl, combine the yogurt, sour cream, Worcestershire sauce, and salt and pepper to taste. Add the onion and garlic mixture, and mix well. Garnish with minced chives.

Serving Suggestion: Serve with flaxseed chips, chopped bell pepper, zucchini, and baby carrots.

Nutrition Facts (amount per serving)	
Calories	161
Total Fat	12 g
Saturated Fat	6 g
Polyunsaturated Fat	0.8 g
Monounsaturated Fat	5 g
Cholesterol	28 mg
Sodium	140 mg
Potassium	247 mg
Total Carbohydrate	9 g
Dietary Fiber	0.1 g
Sugars	6 g
Protein	5 g
Calcium 19% • Magnesium 5%	

Tzatziki Greek Yogurt Sauce
Serves 8 (Makes 2 cups)

2 large cloves garlic, very finely chopped

¼ cup finely diced Persian or English cucumber

¼ cup chopped fresh mint leaves

1¾ cups low-fat plain Greek yogurt

Juice of ½ lemon

1 tablespoon extra virgin olive oil

¼ teaspoon cracked black pepper

⅛ teaspoon sea salt

Combine all the chopped ingredients in a large bowl with the yogurt, lemon juice, and oil. Mix well, and add the salt and pepper. Before serving, let the mixture sit for about 30 minutes to an hour so the flavors can meld.

SERVING TIP

• Enjoy as a dip for raw vegetables or whole wheat pita, as a sauce for wraps or pita sandwiches, or as a dressing for salads.

Nutrition Facts (amount per serving)	
Calories	51
Total Fat	3 g
Saturated Fat	0.8 g
Polyunsaturated Fat	0.3 g
Monounsaturated Fat	2 g
Cholesterol	3 mg
Sodium	57 mg
Potassium	139 mg
Total Carbohydrate	4 g
Dietary Fiber	0.1 g
Sugars	4 g
Protein	3 g
Calcium 10% • Magnesium 3%	

Spinach Artichoke Dip
Serves 4

3 cups spinach

2 (14-ounce) cans artichoke hearts, rinsed, drained, and coarsely
  chopped

1 large clove garlic, finely minced

1 cup low-fat plain Greek yogurt

½ cup low-fat sour cream

¼ teaspoon dried parsley

¼ teaspoon dried basil

½ cup shredded Parmesan cheese, divided

½ cup shredded part-skim mozzarella cheese, divided

⅛ teaspoon sea salt

⅛ teaspoon cracked black pepper

Preheat the oven to 400°F. Fill a medium pot with water, and bring it to a boil. Add the spinach, and after 1 minute drain the spinach in a colander. Let it cool, and then wring the water out by hand. Transfer to a cutting board, and coarsely chop.

In a food processor, add the spinach, artichoke hearts, garlic, yogurt, sour cream, dried herbs, salt, and pepper, and half of both cheeses. Pulse the mixture a few times, to the desired consistency. Process in batches if necessary.

Transfer the mixture to an ovenproof serving dish, and spread it out evenly with a rubber spatula. Top with the rest of the Parmesan and mozzarella. Bake 15 to 20 minutes, or until the cheeses on top completely melt and start to brown. Remove from the oven, and serve immediately.

Serving Suggestion: Serve as a dip with chopped veggies, whole grain crackers, or spread on slices of whole grain baguette.

RECIPE ALTERATIONS
- For chunkier dip, chop all ingredients by hand instead of using a food processor.
- Try serving the dip cold.

Nutrition Facts (amount per serving)	
Calories	263
Total Fat	14 g
Saturated Fat	8 g
Polyunsaturated Fat	0.6 g
Monounsaturated Fat	4 g
Cholesterol	42 mg
Sodium	537 mg
Potassium	666 mg
Total Carbohydrate	18 g
Dietary Fiber	6 g
Sugars	4 g
Protein	20 g
Calcium 55% • Magnesium 20%	

Delicious Bruschetta

Serves 8

1 large whole wheat baguette (about 32 slices)

5 large heirloom tomatoes of various colors, cored and chopped finely

¾ cup finely chopped fresh Italian basil

8–10 fresh mint leaves, finely chopped

2 large cloves garlic, finely minced

½ cup finely minced red onion

¼ cup extra virgin olive oil

⅓ cup balsamic vinegar

¼ teaspoon sea salt

¼ teaspoon cracked black pepper

Preheat the oven to 400°F. Slice the baguette into ¼-inch-thick rounds. Arrange the slices on a cookie sheet and place on the middle rack of the oven. Toast them in the oven for about 5 minutes, or until they become a bit hard and light brown on the edges. Remove them from the oven, and let cool completely.

Drain the chopped tomatoes in a colander. In a large bowl, combine the tomatoes with the herbs, garlic, and onion. Then add the oil and the vinegar, salt, and pepper.

Refrigerate the mixture for at least 30 minutes so the flavors can meld. Top each toasted baguette slice with tomato mixture.

Nutrition Facts *(amount per serving)*	
Calories	221
Total Fat	8 g
Saturated Fat	1 g
Polyunsaturated Fat	1 g
Monounsaturated Fat	5 g
Cholesterol	0 mg
Sodium	396 mg
Potassium	260 mg
Total Carbohydrate	33 g
Dietary Fiber	4 g
Sugars	2 g
Protein	7 g
Calcium 0.9% • Magnesium 3%	

Roasted Zucchini Crostini Dip

Serves 6 (Makes 2 cups)

2 large green zucchini, sliced lengthwise (about ¼ inch thick)

1 large yellow zucchini, sliced lengthwise (about ¼ inch thick)

½ small red onion, coarsely chopped

2 large cloves garlic, whole

¼ cup balsamic vinegar

¼ teaspoon cracked black pepper

¼ teaspoon chile pepper flakes

¼ teaspoon dried basil

⅛ cup extra virgin olive oil

¼ cup grated Parmesan cheese

1–2 tablespoons water, as needed

Preheat the oven to 400°F.

Arrange the sliced zucchini and chopped onion in a roasting pan with the garlic. Drizzle with balsamic vinegar, and season with black pepper, chili pepper flakes, and basil. Roast for 10 to 12 minutes, or until the onion is soft and starting to brown.

Transfer the cooked veggies to a blender or food processor. While blending, slowly drizzle in olive oil, alternating with Parmesan. The result should be a thick spread. For a thinner consistency, add up to 2 tablespoons of water while blending.

Serving Suggestion: Serve as a dip with chopped veggies or sliced whole wheat baguette, or as a topping for chicken or fish.

Nutrition Facts (amount per serving)	
Calories	98
Total Fat	7 g
Saturated Fat	2 g
Polyunsaturated Fat	0.9 g
Monounsaturated Fat	5 g
Cholesterol	3 mg
Sodium	85 mg
Potassium	243 mg
Total Carbohydrate	7 g
Dietary Fiber	2 g
Sugars	1 g
Protein	7 g
Calcium 8% • Magnesium 6%	

Hummus Dip with Curried Pita Chips
Serves 8 (1 serving is 5 tablespoons hummus and 5 chips)

PITA CHIPS

2 100% whole wheat pitas

1–2 tablespoons curry powder

HUMMUS DIP

2 (15-ounce) cans garbanzo beans, rinsed and drained

¼ cup tahini paste

Juice of 2 lemons

2 small cloves garlic, minced

¼ teaspoon sea salt

½ teaspoon cracked black pepper

5 tablespoons extra virgin olive oil, divided

½ teaspoon dried oregano

Preheat the oven to 400°F.

Cut the pitas into 1-inch pieces, and place them on a cookie sheet. Sprinkle with curry powder, and bake for 5 to 8 minutes, or until crunchy.

While the pita chips are baking, make the dip by blending the beans, tahini, lemon juice, garlic, salt, and pepper in a food processor. While processing, drizzle in 4 tablespoons of the oil until there are no large pieces and the hummus is smooth. If a thinner hummus is desired, add 1 tablespoon water at a time while blending. Transfer to a serving dish, top with dried oregano, drizzle with the remaining 1 tablespoon olive oil, and serve with warm curry pita chips.

RECIPE ALTERATION

• Cut down on the amount of oil used by substituting a bit of water to help achieve the desired consistency.

Nutrition Facts (amount per serving)	
Calories	299
Total Fat	14 g
Saturated Fat	2 g
Polyunsaturated Fat	4 g
Monounsaturated Fat	8 g
Cholesterol	0 mg
Sodium	475 mg
Potassium	262 mg
Total Carbohydrate	37 g
Dietary Fiber	7 g
Sugars	1 g
Protein	9 g
Calcium 9% • Magnesium 11%	

Spicy Sun-Roasted Tomato Hummus
Makes 8 (5-tablespoon) servings

2 (15-ounce) cans garbanzo beans, rinsed and drained

¼ cup tahini paste

Juice of 2 lemons

2 large cloves garlic

2 tablespoons sun-roasted tomato slices

1 dried red chile/chile de arbol

½ teaspoon sea salt

½ teaspoon cracked black pepper

5 tablespoons extra virgin olive oil, divided

Place the beans, tahini, lemon juice, garlic, tomato, chile, salt, and pepper in a food processor. While processing, drizzle in the oil until there are no large pieces and the hummus is smooth. If a thinner hummus is desired, add 1 tablespoon water at a time while blending. Transfer to a serving dish, top with dried oregano and a drizzle of olive oil, and serve.

Nutrition Facts *(amount per serving)*	
Calories	262
Total Fat	14 g
Polyunsaturated Fat	2 g
Monounsaturated Fat	8 g
Cholesterol	0 mg
Sodium	471 mg
Potassium	294 mg
Dietary Fiber	6 g
Sugars	1 g
Protein	7 g
Calcium 7% • Magnesium 11%	

Grilled Rustic Corn

Serves 4

4 large ears of corn

¼ teaspoon sea salt

¼ teaspoon cracked black pepper

4 tablespoons extra virgin olive oil

4 large cloves garlic, minced finely

Peel back the husks and remove the silk from each ear of corn. Mix the salt and pepper together in a small bowl. Brush the kernels with oil, and sprinkle each with minced garlic and then the salt and pepper mixture. Fold the husks back over the corn, and grill over low heat until cooked through, 12 to 15 minutes, turning occasionally.

VARIATION

• Remove the husks completely, and wrap each ear of corn in foil to grill.

Nutrition Facts *(amount per serving)*	
Calories	249
Total Fat	16 g
Saturated Fat	2 g
Polyunsaturated Fat	3 g
Monounsaturated Fat	11 g
Cholesterol	0 mg
Sodium	167 mg
Potassium	401 mg
Total Carbohydrate	28 g
Dietary Fiber	4 g
Sugars	5 g
Protein	5 g
Calcium 1% • Magnesium 14%	

Grilled Sweet Potato Steak Fries
Serves 4

1 pound (about 4 medium) sweet potatoes, unpeeled

4 tablespoons extra virgin olive oil

½ teaspoon ground cumin

½ teaspoon cayenne pepper

¼ teaspoon cracked black pepper

¼ teaspoon sea salt

Fill a large pot with water, and bring it to a boil. Add the sweet potatoes, and boil 10 to 12 minutes, or until an inserted fork glides in easily but the potato is slightly firm in the center. Strain the potatoes, and let them cool. Once cooled, cut them in half lengthwise and then into ½-inch-thick pieces lengthwise. The skin may peel a bit, but keep it on as it provides nutritious fiber. Brush oil onto each slice, and sprinkle with cumin, cayenne, and black pepper. Arrange on the grill, and cook 1 to 2 minutes per side. Remove from the heat, season with salt, and serve.

RECIPE ALTERATION

• Bake oiled and seasoned potato slices in a preheated 400°F oven until golden brown, turning occasionally, about 20 minutes, or until an inserted fork glides in easily.

Nutrition Facts *(amount per serving)*	
Calories	258
Total Fat	14 g
Saturated Fat	2 g
Polyunsaturated Fat	2 g
Monounsaturated Fat	10 g
Cholesterol	0 mg
Sodium	166 mg
Potassium	166 mg
Total Carbohydrate	32 g
Dietary Fiber	4 g
Sugars	0 g
Protein	2 g
Calcium 3% • Magnesium 3%	

Grilled Asparagus
Serves 4

1 pound asparagus
5 tablespoons extra virgin olive oil
Grated zest of 1 large lemon
Juice of ½ lemon
3 large cloves garlic, minced
¼ teaspoon sea salt
⅛ teaspoon cracked black pepper

Cut off and discard the fibrous thick ends of the asparagus spears. In a large baking dish or rimmed cookie sheets, lay the spears in a single, even layer, and drizzle with oil. Roll the spears in the oil to coat evenly. Add the lemon zest, lemon juice, garlic, salt, and pepper over the top. Roll the spears again to coat all sides with the seasonings. Place on a hot grill, and rotate the spears constantly so they do not burn. Grill for about 2 minutes, and return to marinating pan to serve.

Nutrition Facts (amount per serving)	
Calories	163
Total Fat	18 g
Saturated Fat	3 g
Polyunsaturated Fat	3 g
Monounsaturated Fat	13 g
Cholesterol	0 mg
Sodium	292 mg
Potassium	119 mg
Total Carbohydrate	3 g
Dietary Fiber	0.9 g
Sugars	0 g
Protein	1 g
Calcium 1% • Magnesium 7%	

Grilled Collard Greens

Serves 4

1 pound collard greens
4 tablespoons red wine vinegar
5 tablespoons extra virgin olive oil
¼ teaspoon sea salt
¼ teaspoon cracked black pepper

Cut off the thick ends of the stems, and then wash the greens and pat them completely dry. Lay each leaf directly on a hot grill. After 30 seconds, flip each leaf over. When they start to wither and blacken, remove the leaves, place them in a large pot, and cover with a lid. After all the leaves have been grilled, let them sit in the covered pot for about 5 minutes to continue steaming. Remove the leaves from the pot, and cut them into 2-inch-wide pieces. Place them back in the pot, top with the vinegar, oil, salt, and pepper to taste. Serve warm or chilled.

Nutrition Facts (amount per serving)	
Calories	135
Total Fat	14 g
Saturated Fat	2 g
Polyunsaturated Fat	2 g
Monounsaturated Fat	10 g
Cholesterol	0 mg
Sodium	156 mg
Potassium	80 mg
Total Carbohydrate	3 g
Dietary Fiber	2 g
Sugars	0.2 g
Protein	1 g
Calcium 6% • Magnesium 1%	

Not Your Mama's Green Bean Casserole
Serves 6

4½ cups green beans

¼ cup chopped shallots

2 large cloves garlic, finely minced

⅛ teaspoon sea salt

Cracked black pepper

2 tablespoons extra virgin olive oil

1 large lemon

¾ cup chopped toasted hazelnuts

Cut off and discard both ends of the green beans. Bring a large pot of water to a boil, and add the beans, cooking them at a boil for only about 5 minutes. Drain them in a colander, and then rinse with ice water. (This stops the cooking process so that the beans stay bright green and crispy.)

Heat the oil in a large pan over medium heat. Once the pan is hot, add the shallots and garlic, and cook for a few minutes, until they begin to brown. Add the green beans, and season with the salt and pepper to taste. Grate the zest of the lemon into the mixture. Then cut the lemon in half, and add its juice. Cook for another 5 to 7 minutes, or until heated through.

Transfer the green bean mixture to a large serving dish, and top with the chopped hazelnuts. Serve immediately.

Nutrition Facts (amount per serving)	
Calories	181
Total Fat	15 g
Saturated Fat	2 g
Polyunsaturated Fat	2 g
Monounsaturated Fat	11 g
Cholesterol	0 mg
Sodium	55 mg
Potassium	340 g
Total Carbohydrate	12 g
Dietary Fiber	5 g
Sugars	1 g
Protein	5 g
Calcium 7% • Magnesium 13%	

Brussels Sprouts Casserole
Serves 6

1½ pounds (6 cups) Brussels sprouts

2 thick slices pancetta, diced

2 tablespoons chopped shallot

2 large cloves garlic, finely minced

½ cup toasted pine nuts, divided

½ teaspoon cracked black pepper

Preheat the oven to 400°F.

Bring a large pot of water to a boil. Peel off and discard the outer leaves of the Brussels sprouts and trim the stems. Halve the Brussels sprouts, and add to the boiling water. Boil 10 to 15 minutes, or until the sprouts are easily pierced with a fork. Drain and set aside.

Trim the fat from the pancetta before dicing. Heat a large saucepan over medium heat, and add the pancetta. Sauté until brown and crispy, about 4 to 5 minutes. Transfer the pancetta to paper towels to drain. Add the garlic and shallots and half the pine nuts to the same pan. Cook until the nuts turn light brown, about 1 to 2 minutes, and then add the Brussels sprouts. Cook them for an additional 2 to 3 minutes so they absorb the pancetta and garlic flavors. Pour the mixture into an 8- by 8-inch baking dish, season with pepper, and bake for 10 to 15 minutes, or until the tops of the Brussels sprouts brown. Remove from the oven, and top with the remaining pine nuts before serving.

Nutrition Facts (amount per serving)	
Calories	128
Total Fat	9 g
Saturated Fat	0.9 g
Polyunsaturated Fat	4 g
Monounsaturated Fat	2 g
Cholesterol	2 mg
Sodium	56 mg
Potassium	425 mg
Total Carbohydrate	10 g
Dietary Fiber	4 g
Sugars	2 g
Protein	5 g
Calcium 4% • Magnesium 12%	

Kale and Butternut Squash Sauté
Serves 6

1 pound kale

1 pound (4 cups) pre-cut butternut squash

2 tablespoons extra virgin olive oil

1 tablespoon shallot, finely chopped

2 large cloves garlic, minced

½ cup toasted pine nuts

Pinch of chile pepper flakes

⅛ teaspoon sea salt

⅛ teaspoon cracked black pepper

4 tablespoons grated Pecorino Romano cheese

Chop off and discard the rough ends of the kale. Wash, dry thoroughly, and coarsely chop the kale. Heat the oil in a large pan over medium heat. Add the squash, and cook 15 to 20 minutes, or until browned and an inserted fork easily glides in. Add the kale, cook for 1 minute, and then add the shallot, garlic, chile flakes, salt, and pepper. Sauté for 3 more minutes, add the pine nuts, and cook for another minute. Transfer the mixture to a serving dish, and top with Pecorino Romano.

RECIPE ALTERATION

• Pecorino Romano is salty, hard, and dry like Parmesan cheese, but is made from sheep's milk. If you cannot find it in stores, substitute with Parmesan.

Nutrition Facts (amount per serving)	
Calories	144
Total Fat	7 g
Saturated Fat	2 g
Polyunsaturated Fat	1 g
Monounsaturated Fat	4 g
Cholesterol	3 mg
Sodium	133 mg
Potassium	627 mg
Total Carbohydrate	21 g
Dietary Fiber	6 g
Sugars	1 g
Protein	5 g
Calcium 19% • Magnesium 15%	

Sautéed Greens with Cannellini Beans
Serves 4

1 pound mixed greens (such as mustard greens, kale, collard greens, and chard), coarsely chopped

3 tablespoons extra virgin olive oil

½ small red onion, finely chopped

2 large cloves garlic, minced

¼ teaspoon chile pepper flakes

⅛ teaspoon sea salt

⅛ teaspoon cracked black pepper

3 tablespoons water or chicken broth

½ tablespoon lemon zest

1 (15-ounce) can cannellini beans, rinsed and drained

¼ cup toasted pine nuts

Wash the greens, and dry them thoroughly. Heat the oil in a large sauté pan over medium heat, and add the onion. After a minute, add the garlic and chile pepper flakes, and once the garlic becomes fragrant, add the greens, and season with salt and pepper. They will reduce in size quite a bit. Toss frequently to avoid burning. Add the water or broth, and cover with a lid. After about 3 minutes, remove the lid, add the beans, and cook for another 2 minutes to heat the beans through. Transfer to a serving dish, and top with the toasted pine nuts.

Nutrition Facts *(amount per serving)*	
Calories	302
Total Fat	17 g
Saturated Fat	2 g
Polyunsaturated Fat	5 g
Monounsaturated Fat	9 g
Cholesterol	0 mg
Sodium	67 mg
Potassium	769 g
Total Carbohydrate	31 g
Dietary Fiber	8 g
Sugars	0.9 g
Protein	11 g
Calcium 17% • Magnesium 23%	

Roasted Cauliflower
Serves 4

4 cups cauliflower florets (1 small head cauliflower)

4 tablespoons extra virgin olive oil

3 large cloves garlic, minced

½ teaspoon chile pepper flakes

Grated zest of 1 large lemon

⅛ teaspoon sea salt

⅛ teaspoon cracked black pepper

3 tablespoons chopped fresh basil

Preheat the oven to 400°F. Remove and discard the stems and core of the cauliflower. Place the cauliflower head in an 8- by 8-inch baking dish. Drizzle with oil, and then sprinkle on the garlic, chile pepper flakes, lemon zest, salt, and pepper. Shake the pan a bit so that the oil spreads and the ingredients cover the cauliflower. Bake 15 to 20 minutes, shaking the pan after 10 minutes to prevent the cauliflower from sticking. Remove from the heat, top with fresh basil, and serve immediately.

Nutrition Facts (amount per serving)	
Calories	150
Total Fat	14 g
Saturated Fat	2 g
Polyunsaturated Fat	2 g
Monounsaturated Fat	10 g
Cholesterol	0 mg
Sodium	69 mg
Potassium	324 mg
Total Carbohydrate	6 g
Dietary Fiber	3 g
Sugars	0.1 g
Protein	2.2 g
Calcium 3% • Magnesium 4%	

Sautéed Vegetables
Serves 4

1 pound asparagus

2 tablespoons extra virgin olive oil

¼ white onion, chopped

1 large clove garlic, chopped

1 large green zucchini, sliced

1 large yellow zucchini, sliced

1 tablespoon chopped fresh parsley

Juice of ½ lemon

⅛ teaspoon sea salt

⅛ teaspoon cracked black pepper

Cut off and discard the tough ends of the asparagus spears. Heat the oil in a large pan over medium heat. Add the onion and garlic, and after about a minute add the asparagus. After 2 to 3 minutes, add the zucchini, parsley, and lemon juice. Cook for 4 to 5 more minutes, and then remove from the heat. Season with salt and pepper to taste before serving.

Nutrition Facts (amount per serving)	
Calories	108
Total Fat	7 g
Saturated Fat	1 g
Polyunsaturated Fat	1 g
Monounsaturated Fat	5 g
Cholesterol	0 mg
Sodium	6 mg
Potassium	482 mg
Total Carbohydrate	12 g
Dietary Fiber	4 g
Sugars	2 g
Protein	3 g
Calcium 4% • Magnesium 9%	

Grilled Eggplant and Zucchini
Serves 4

1 large eggplant, sliced into ½-inch rounds

2 zucchini, sliced lengthwise

¼ teaspoon sea salt, divided

⅛ teaspoon cracked black pepper

¼ teaspoon dried parsley

¼ teaspoon dried basil

¼ teaspoon dried oregano

6 tablespoons balsamic vinegar

4 tablespoons extra virgin olive oil

Lay the sliced eggplant on paper towels, and sprinkle each slice with a pinch of salt to pull out excess moisture. After 10 to 15 minutes, pat the slices dry with paper towels. Arrange the eggplant and zucchini on a cookie sheet with edges on it. Sprinkle pepper and dried herbs over the veggies, and drizzle with vinegar and oil. Grill the veggies on a hot grill or grill pan for 4 to 6 minutes, flipping halfway through. Remove from the grill or grill pan and serve.

Nutrition Facts *(amount per serving)*	
Calories	183
Total Fat	14 g
Saturated Fat	2 g
Polyunsaturated Fat	2 g
Monounsaturated Fat	10 g
Cholesterol	0 mg
Sodium	160 mg
Potassium	533 mg
Total Carbohydrate	15 g
Dietary Fiber	5 g
Sugars	2 g
Protein	2 g
Calcium 3% • Magnesium 10%	

Cilantro-Lime Brown Rice
Serves 2

¾ cup uncooked brown rice

1½ cups low-sodium vegetable broth

Juice of 1 lime

1 tablespoon chopped fresh cilantro

In a small pot, bring the rice and broth to a boil over high heat. Cover the pot, reduce the heat to low, and simmer for about 40 minutes or until the rice is cooked and the liquid absorbed. Once the rice is fully cooked, fluff with a fork, add the lime juice and cilantro, and stir to mix well.

Nutrition Facts (amount per serving)	
Calories	56
Total Fat	0.3 g
Saturated Fat	0.1 g
Polyunsaturated Fat	0.1 g
Cholesterol	0 mg
Sodium	174 mg
Potassium	40 mg
Total Carbohydrate	12 g
Dietary Fiber	1 g
Sugars	1 g
Protein	1 g
Calcium 2% • Magnesium 4%	

Plain and Simple Couscous

Serves 4 (Makes 2 cups)

¾ cup uncooked whole wheat couscous
¾ cup low-sodium vegetable broth
1 tablespoon extra virgin olive oil
⅛ teaspoon cracked black pepper

Heat a small pot over medium heat, and add the couscous to toast it until lightly browned and fragrant. Toast for about 2 minutes, stirring constantly. Temporarily place the couscous in a bowl. Add the broth to the pot, and bring it to a boil. Then add the couscous, and remove the pot from the heat. Cover, and let sit for 5 minutes. Fluff the couscous with a fork, drizzle with oil, and sprinkle with pepper before serving.

Nutrition Facts *(amount per serving)*	
Calories	84
Total Fat	4 g
Saturated Fat	0.9 g
Polyunsaturated Fat	0.5 g
Monounsaturated Fat	3 g
Cholesterol	0 mg
Sodium	147 mg
Potassium	0 mg
Total Carbohydrate	11 g
Dietary Fiber	0.9 g
Sugars	3 g
Protein	2 g
Calcium 0.4% • Magnesium 0%	

Quinoa and Veggies
Serves 4

1 cup uncooked quinoa

2 cups vegetable broth

2 tablespoons extra virgin olive oil

¼ cup chopped red onion

1 small clove garlic, minced

1 large zucchini, chopped into small cubes

⅛ teaspoon chile pepper flakes

3 cups spinach

Rinse the quinoa (if not prerinsed). Place the quinoa and broth in a large pot, and bring to a boil. Reduce heat to low, and cover with lid slightly ajar. Simmer on low for about 15 to 20 minutes, or until liquid is absorbed and the quinoa has uncoiled and is al dente.

Heat the oil in a separate pan over medium heat. Add the onion, garlic, and zucchini, and cook until the onion is translucent. Season with chile flakes, and transfer the veggies to the pot with the cooked quinoa. Add the spinach, stir, and cover the pot. Let sit for 5 minutes. Serve warm.

Nutrition Facts (amount per serving)	
Calories	265
Total Fat	10 g
Saturated Fat	1 g
Polyunsaturated Fat	1 g
Monounsaturated Fat	5 g
Cholesterol	0 mg
Sodium	251 mg
Potassium	260 mg
Total Carbohydrate	37 g
Dietary Fiber	5 g
Sugars	5 g
Protein	8 g
Calcium 4% • Magnesium 7%	

Healthier Stuffing*
Serves 6

7 to 8 slices whole wheat bread, cut in 1-inch cubes (4 cups)

4 spicy Italian turkey or chicken sausages

3 tablespoons extra virgin olive oil

2 ribs celery, chopped

2 large cloves garlic, minced

1 medium white onion, chopped

1 cup thinly sliced cremini mushrooms

½ cup white wine

2–3 cups low-sodium chicken broth

2 tablespoons chopped fresh parsley

3-4 large fresh sage leaves, finely minced

1 cup chopped walnuts

1 cup dried cranberries

To make the bread cubes, preheat the oven to 375°F. You can use a small whole wheat or whole grain loaf or use whole wheat or whole grain sandwich bread, but please note that you only need 4 cups of cubed bread for this recipe. Arrange the cubes evenly on a cookie sheet, and toast in the oven for about 5 minutes. Shake the pan to move the pieces around a bit, and bake for another 5 minutes, or until most pieces are toasted and crunchy on top. Remove from the oven, and put in a large container. Cover with a cloth and leave out at room temperature overnight, so that the cubes get stale and hard.

To make the stuffing, remove the casings from the sausages, and crumble the meat. Heat the oil in a large pan over medium heat. Add the sausage and celery, and cook for about 6 to 8 minutes. Remove the mixture with a slotted spoon and drain on several layers of paper towels. To the same pan, add the garlic, onion, and mushrooms. Add the wine, and scrape the bottom of the pan to combine flavors. Simmer for a couple minutes, and then add the meat mixture and bread cubes, a handful at a time. Add 2 cups of broth, parsley, sage, walnuts, and cranberries. Cover the pan, and cook on low until the mixture begins bubbling, about 5 to 6 minutes. Add the remaining cup of broth if a wetter stuffing is preferred. Remove from the heat, and serve.

RECIPE ALTERATION
• Baking is not necessary. But if desired, add ½ cup more broth, transfer to a 9- by 13-inch baking dish, and bake at 350°F for about 20 minutes, or until the top of the stuffing is browned and crunchy.

Nutrition Facts (amount per serving)	
Calories	403
Total Fat	18 g
Saturated Fat	2 g
Polyunsaturated Fat	10 g
Monounsaturated Fat	3 g
Cholesterol	17 mg
Sodium	589 mg
Potassium	321g
Total Carbohydrate	50 g
Dietary Fiber	7 g
Sugars	21 g
Protein	13 g
Calcium 10% • Magnesium 17%	

* This recipe must be started at least 1 day in advance to make your own whole wheat bread cubes

Desserts

Everyone loves dessert! And even when you're counting calories, it's important to allow yourself a sweet treat here and there. These dessert recipes offer satisfyingly sweet deliciousness while remaining health conscious. Keep in mind that when making dessert at home you can control exactly how much sugar and other ingredients go into it, whereas you don't really know what's in store-bought or restaurant desserts. Enjoy!

Berry Sundae
Serves 6

1½ cups coarsely chopped strawberries
1½ cups blueberries
1½ cups raspberries
1½ tablespoons balsamic vinegar
Pinch of cracked black pepper
1½ teaspoons grated lemon zest
1½ teaspoons grated orange zest
Juice of ½ orange
½ teaspoon vanilla extract
3 cups low-fat plain Greek yogurt
6 tablespoons sliced toasted almonds

Place all ingredients except the yogurt and almonds in a large pot over medium heat, and cook until the liquid begins to bubble. Decrease the heat to low, and boil the mixture for about 15 minutes, or until it thickens. The berries will naturally fall apart, leaving a slightly chunky sauce. For a smoother sauce, crush the berries with a fork or masher. Remove from the heat. Place ½ cup of yogurt into six bowls, and top with sauce and toasted almonds.

Nutrition Facts *(amount per serving)*	
Calories	163
Total Fat	4 g
Saturated Fat	2 g
Polyunsaturated Fat	0.7 g
Monounsaturated Fat	1 g
Cholesterol	5 mg
Sodium	47 mg
Potassium	353 mg
Total Carbohydrate	20 g
Dietary Fiber	5 g
Sugars	10 g
Protein	14 g
Calcium 13% • Magnesium 6%	

Grilled Apricots with Cinnamon

Serves 4

4 large apricots, halved and pitted

1 tablespoon extra virgin olive oil

¼ teaspoon ground cinnamon

Brush both sides of each apricot half with oil, and place flat side down on a heated grill or grill pan. Grill for about 4 minutes, turn the apricot halves over, and cook for a few more minutes, until soft. Remove the apricots from the grill, and sprinkle with cinnamon. Enjoy warm or chilled.

Nutrition Facts (amount per serving)	
Calories	47
Total Fat	4 g
Saturated Fat	0.5 g
Polyunsaturated Fat	0.5 g
Monounsaturated Fat	3 g
Cholesterol	0 mg
Sodium	0.4 mg
Potassium	91 mg
Total Carbohydrate	4 g
Dietary Fiber	0.8 g
Sugars	3 g
Protein	0.5 g
Calcium 0.6% • Magnesium 0.9%	

Grilled Peaches with Ricotta Stuffing and Balsamic Glaze

Serves 4

4 large peaches, halved and pitted

1 tablespoon extra virgin olive oil

1 cup low-fat ricotta cheese

¼ teaspoon ground cinnamon

⅛ teaspoon ground nutmeg

2 tablespoons low-fat milk

2 tablespoons Balsamic Glaze (page 89)

Brush both sides of each peach half with oil, and place flat side down on a heated grill or grill pan. Grill for about 4 minutes, turn the peach halves over, and cook for a few more minutes, until soft. While the peaches are grilling, mix the ricotta, milk, cinnamon, and nutmeg in a small bowl, stirring to incorporate flavors evenly. Remove the peaches from the grill, and scoop ¼ cup of the ricotta mixture into the center of each peach half. Drizzle balsamic glaze over each, and serve.

Nutrition Facts (amount per serving)	
Calories	191
Total Fat	9 g
Saturated Fat	4 g
Polyunsaturated Fat	0.7 g
Monounsaturated Fat	4 g
Cholesterol	20 mg
Sodium	83 mg
Potassium	387 mg
Total Carbohydrate	22 g
Dietary Fiber	3 g
Sugars	0.6 g
Protein	8 g
Calcium 19% • Magnesium 5%	

Grilled Pineapple
Serves 6

1 large pineapple, sliced into rounds and cored

Cut the pineapple by laying it on its side and cutting off the top and bottom. Stand it up on its newly flat base. Working in a circular direction, cut the skin off in a downward motion, starting from the top and going to the base. Be careful not to cut off too much of the fruit with the skin. Once the skin has been removed, cut away any brown spots. Then lay it lengthwise again, and slice rounds to desired thickness. Use a cookie cutter or knife to cut out the inedible core at the center of each round.

Place the pineapple rings directly onto a hot grill. Grill for about 3 minutes, or until char marks appear. Then turn the rings over, and grill for another 2 to 3 minutes. Serve warm or chilled.

Nutrition Facts *(amount per serving)*	
Calories	39
Total Fat	0.4 g
Saturated Fat	0 g
Polyunsaturated Fat	0.1 g
Monounsaturated Fat	0.1 g
Cholesterol	0 mg
Sodium	0.8 mg
Potassium	89 mg
Total Carbohydrate	10 g
Dietary Fiber	1 g
Sugars	8 g
Protein	0.3 g
Calcium 0.6% • Magnesium 3%	

Red Sangria

Serves 8

1 (750 mL) bottle Spanish red table wine

¼ cup brandy

¼ cup Cointreau

½ cup orange juice

1 cup pomegranate juice

2 oranges, thinly sliced

2 Granny Smith apples, thinly sliced

1½ cups seltzer, mineral water, or club soda

   In a large pitcher, stir together the wine, brandy, Cointreau, and fruit juices. Add the sliced fruit, and chill in the refrigerator for at least 30 minutes before serving. Add the seltzer, mineral water, or club soda just before serving.

Nutrition Facts *(amount per serving)*	
Calories	173
Total Fat	0.3 g
Saturated Fat	0 g
Polyunsaturated Fat	0 g
Monounsaturated Fat	0 g
Cholesterol	0 mg
Sodium	9 mg
Potassium	272 mg
Total Carbohydrate	21 g
Dietary Fiber	2 g
Sugars	17 g
Protein	0.9 g
Calcium 4% • Magnesium 5%	

White Sangria
Serves 8

1 (750 mL) bottle chilled white wine, such as sauvignon blanc
  or pinot grigio
¼ cup brandy
2 large firm peaches, halved, pitted, and thinly sliced
3 Bartlett pears, thinly sliced
1 cup raspberries
15–20 fresh mint leaves
1½ cups seltzer, mineral water, or club soda

In a large pitcher, stir together the wine and brandy. Add
the fruits and mint leaves, and chill in the refrigerator for
at least 30 minutes before serving. Add the seltzer, mineral
water, or club soda just before serving.

Nutrition Facts *(amount per serving)*	
Calories	139
Total Fat	0.4 g
Saturated Fat	0 g
Polyunsaturated Fat	0.1 g
Monounsaturated Fat	0.1 g
Cholesterol	0 mg
Sodium	5 mg
Potassium	254 mg
Total Carbohydrate	16 g
Dietary Fiber	3 g
Sugars	0 g
Protein	0.8 g
Calcium 3% • Magnesium 5%	

Cucumber-Watermelon Cooler
Serves 4 (Makes 5 cups)

5 cups chopped seedless watermelon

1 cup chopped unpeeled cucumber

10 fresh mint leaves

Juice of ½ lime

Blend the watermelon and cucumber in the blender, in batches if necessary. Add the mint and lime juice in the last blend. Serve chilled as a beverage or summer soup, or freeze in Popsicle molds for a light treat.

Nutrition Facts (amount per serving)	
Calories	66
Total Fat	0.9 g
Saturated Fat	0.1 g
Polyunsaturated Fat	0.3 g
Monounsaturated Fat	0.3 g
Cholesterol	0 mg
Sodium	5 mg
Potassium	267 mg
Total Carbohydrate	15 g
Dietary Fiber	1 g
Sugars	13 g
Protein	2 g
Calcium 2% • Magnesium 6%	

Brie-Stuffed Apples
Serves 4

1 small wedge Brie cheese

4 large Gala apples

1½ tablespoons lemon juice, divided

⅛ teaspoon ground nutmeg

¼ teaspoon ground cinnamon

¼ cup black currants

¼ cup chopped walnuts

2 tablespoons brown sugar, divided

Preheat the oven to 375°F. Place the Brie wedge in the freezer for 10 minutes (to make for easier chopping later).

To core each apple, cut in a wide, circular motion all the way around the top of the apple toward the base. Pop the top off, and cut off and discard any tough pieces connected to the core. Using a teaspoon, scoop out most of the inside of the apple, along with the remaining seeds. Discard the seeds, and coarsely chop the apple flesh (about 1½ cups). Set aside in a medium bowl. Brush the inside of each cored apple with lemon juice. Reserve the remaining lemon juice.

Remove the Brie from the freezer, and cut into small cubes, about the same size as the apple pieces (about ½ cup). Add the Brie and remaining ingredients to the apple mixture, and top with remaining lemon juice. Mix to incorporate the ingredients evenly. Using a tablespoon, stuff each cored apple with the apple-cheese mixture until it reaches just above the top of the apple (so it looks overstuffed). Sprinkle with brown sugar.

Place the stuffed apples in a 9-inch round cake pan, and add about ½ inch of water to the pan. Cover with foil, and bake for about 20 to 25 minutes, or until you can easily pierce the apples with a fork or toothpick.

Nutrition Facts *(amount per serving)*	
Calories	242
Total Fat	10 g
Saturated Fat	4 g
Polyunsaturated Fat	4 g
Monounsaturated Fat	2 g
Cholesterol	18 mg
Sodium	115 mg
Potassium	245 mg
Total Carbohydrate	35 g
Dietary Fiber	6 g
Sugars	27 g
Protein	5 g
Calcium 5% • Magnesium 4%	

Spiced Applesauce
Serves 4

5 large apples, peeled

¼ cup water

1 cinnamon stick

3 cloves

Zest of ½ lemon

½ teaspoon ground ginger

Cut the peeled apples into wedges, and discard the cores. Place the apples, water, and spices in a large pot. Cover, and simmer over low heat for about 20 minutes, or until the apples have absorbed the liquid and are fluffy to the touch. Remove the cinnamon stick and cloves, and mash the apples with a potato masher or fork to the desired consistency. For super smooth applesauce, transfer the mixture to a blender, and blend in small batches.

Serving suggestion: Top vanilla ice cream with warm applesauce and crumbled pecans or walnuts or enjoy as is.

Nutrition Facts *(amount per serving)*	
Calories	157
Total Fat	0.4 g
Saturated Fat	0.2 g
Polyunsaturated Fat	0.2 g
Monounsaturated Fat	0 g
Cholesterol	0 mg
Sodium	0.1 mg
Potassium	308 mg
Total Carbohydrate	41 g
Dietary Fiber	7 g
Sugars	27 g
Protein	0.4 g
Calcium 2% • Magnesium 4%	

Sweet Potato Dessert
Serves 1

1 small or ½ large sweet potato
½ cup low-fat vanilla yogurt
¼ teaspoon ground cinnamon
2 tablespoons sliced almonds

Preheat the oven to 400°F. Pierce the sweet potato with a fork in several places, wrap in foil, and place on a cookie sheet to catch any juicy drippings. Bake for about 30 to 40 minutes, or until the sweet potato is soft and squishy to the touch. Remove from the oven, unwrap, and place in a bowl. Cut open down the middle, and top with the yogurt, cinnamon, and almonds.

Nutrition Facts (amount per serving)	
Calories	179
Total Fat	6 g
Saturated Fat	7 g
Polyunsaturated Fat	1 g
Monounsaturated Fat	3 g
Cholesterol	7 mg
Sodium	108 mg
Potassium	633 mg
Total Carbohydrate	23 g
Dietary Fiber	3 g
Sugars	14 g
Protein	9 g
Calcium 27% • Magnesium 13%	

Brandied Peaches and Apples with Caramel Pecans

Serves 6

¼ cup dried berries (any mix such as golden raisins, cherries, and cranberries)

½ cup brandy

2 tablespoons extra virgin olive oil

4 ripe peaches, halved, pitted, and cubed

2 large Gala apples, unpeeled, cored, and cubed

1 tablespoon grated orange zest

½ teaspoon ground cinnamon

⅛ teaspoon ground ginger

2 tablespoons orange liqueur

CARAMEL PECANS

½ cup chopped pecans

3 tablespoons brown sugar

1 tablespoon water

In a medium bowl, soak the dried berries in the brandy while you prepare the remaining ingredients.

For the caramel pecans, in a dry skillet, toast the pecans over medium heat until they're lightly browned and you can smell them toasting. Add the brown sugar, and mix well. Once the sugar starts to melt add the water, and stir quickly so that the mixture is evenly coated. Immediately move the mixture to a large sheet of waxed paper, and spread out in a thin layer. Let it sit for 5 minutes, or until it hardens. Peel off the waxed paper, and crumble by hand.

Heat the oil in a large sauté pan, and add the peaches and apples. Add the orange zest and cinnamon, and toss so the fruit is evenly coated and begins to caramelize. Add the brandied berry mixture, and simmer for about 30 seconds. Add the orange liqueur and mix. Serve hot in individual bowls and top with the caramel pecans.

Serving suggestion: Top with a dollop of homemade Whipped Cream (page 228) for an extra treat.

Nutrition Facts *(amount per serving)*	
Calories	274
Total Fat	12 g
Saturated Fat	1 g
Polyunsaturated Fat	3 g
Monounsaturated Fat	7 g
Cholesterol	0 mg
Sodium	3 mg
Potassium	427 mg
Total Carbohydrate	37 g
Dietary Fiber	6 g
Sugars	18 g
Protein	2 g
Calcium 2% • Magnesium 6%	

Macerated Strawberries with Homemade Whipped Cream
Serves 6

2 cups sliced strawberries

2 tablespoons balsamic vinegar

3 tablespoons brown sugar

¼ teaspoon cracked black pepper

WHIPPED CREAM

¼ cup cold heavy whipping cream

½ teaspoon vanilla extract

2 tablespoons brown sugar

1½ teaspoons grated orange zest

Place the strawberry slices in a large bowl. Add the vinegar and sugar, mix together, and let sit for at least 30 minutes so that the flavors meld and a syrupy sauce forms.

In a separate large bowl, whip the cold cream and vanilla with a hand mixer at high speed until bubbles form and the cream starts thickening. Add the sugar gradually while mixing and continue mixing until stiff peaks form. Fold in the orange zest with a spatula.

Dish the strawberries into small bowls, and top with black pepper and whipped cream. Drizzle some of the syrup from the strawberry bowl over the top.

FUN FACTS

• Brown sugar is not absolutely necessary for the macerated strawberries, but it does help to balance the tanginess of the balsamic vinegar as well as contribute to a delicious, and relatively healthy, syrup.

- Although heavy whipping cream is not low in calories, a little goes a long way, and it's actually a healthier choice than processed whipped toppings. You know exactly what you're putting into this recipe!
- Add 2 tablespoons of orange liqueur to the strawberry mixture for an "adults only" dessert.

Nutrition Facts (amount per serving)	
Calories	82
Total Fat	4 g
Saturated Fat	2 g
Polyunsaturated Fat	0.2 g
Monounsaturated Fat	1 g
Cholesterol	14 mg
Sodium	9 mg
Potassium	119 mg
Total Carbohydrate	15 g
Dietary Fiber	1 g
Sugars	13 g
Protein	0.5 g
Calcium 2% • Magnesium 2%	

Mexican Fruit Salad
Serves 4

½ cantaloupe, cut into bite-sized cubes (about 2 cups)

5 large strawberries, sliced

2 kiwifruit, peeled, halved, and sliced

1 large banana, sliced

½ cup halved green and red grapes

1 cup low-fat cottage cheese

¼ cup raisins

3 tablespoons honey

½ cup low-sugar granola

Place all cut fruit in a large bowl. Top with cottage cheese and raisins, and then drizzle honey over the top. Let sit for 30 minutes in the refrigerator, and then toss before spooning into serving bowls. Top each serving with granola.

HELPFUL TIPS

• This healthy dessert also makes a great breakfast or snack. Just don't add extra honey, as the fruit already contains enough sugar.

• If you're using store-bought granola, be sure to read the nutrition label carefully. Packaged granola is often packed with added sugar and other unnecessary sweeteners. Be sure to find the most natural kind with the least amount of sugar.

Nutrition Facts *(amount per serving)*	
Calories	295
Total Fat	5 g
Saturated Fat	1 g
Polyunsaturated Fat	2 g
Monounsaturated Fat	1 g
Cholesterol	2 mg
Sodium	251 mg
Potassium	561 mg
Total Carbohydrate	56 g
Dietary Fiber	5 g
Sugars	36 g
Protein	11 g
Calcium 8% • Magnesium 15%	

Sweet Carrot and Apple Salad

Serves 4

2 large Granny Smith apples, cut into matchsticks (about 1½ cups)

2 large carrots, cut into matchsticks (about 1½ cups)

1 cup low-fat plain Greek yogurt

¼ cup raisins

1 teaspoon ground cinnamon

¼ teaspoon ground ginger

¼ teaspoon curry powder

Mix the apples and carrots into the yogurt, and stir in the remaining ingredients. Let sit for at least 30 minutes before serving.

Serving suggestion: Use as a topping for waffles or pancakes.

Nutrition Facts (amount per serving)	
Calories	117
Total Fat	0.7 g
Saturated Fat	0 g
Polyunsaturated Fat	0.1 g
Monounsaturated Fat	0 g
Cholesterol	0 mg
Sodium	50 mg
Potassium	216 mg
Total Carbohydrate	26 g
Dietary Fiber	4 g
Sugars	19 g
Protein	6 g
Calcium 9% • Magnesium 4%	

Banana Chocolate Dessert Smoothie
Serves 2

1 medium frozen banana, chopped

¾ cup unsweetened almond milk

¼ cup water

1½ tablespoons unsweetened cocoa powder

⅛ teaspoon ground cinnamon

1 tablespoon raw, unsalted almond butter

3 drops almond extract

3–4 ice cubes

Sprig of fresh mint

Place all ingredients except the mint in a blender, and blend on high for about a minute. For a thicker, slushier smoothie, add more ice. Garnish with fresh mint.

Nutrition Facts *(amount per serving)*	
Calories	139
Total Fat	7 g
Saturated Fat	1 g
Polyunsaturated Fat	1 g
Monounsaturated Fat	3 g
Cholesterol	0 mg
Sodium	71 mg
Potassium	464 mg
Total Carbohydrate	21 g
Dietary Fiber	4 g
Sugars	9 g
Protein	3 g
Calcium 11% • Magnesium 18%	

Mini Banana Split
Serves 2

3 tablespoons dark chocolate chips or chopped dark chocolate

1 large banana, sliced

1 cup low-fat frozen yogurt

¼ cup chopped strawberries

¼ cup chopped pineapple

2 tablespoons toasted chopped almonds

Place the chocolate in a small, microwave-safe bowl, and microwave for 10 seconds. Stir the chocolate, and repeat the process until the chocolate is fully melted. Assemble banana splits in two small ramekins by arranging banana slices around the edge of each dish, and then scooping frozen yogurt into the center, in the middle of the bananas. Add the toppings, and drizzle each with chocolate.

Nutrition Facts *(amount per serving)*	
Calories	332
Total Fat	11 g
Saturated Fat	5 g
Polyunsaturated Fat	1 g
Monounsaturated Fat	2 g
Cholesterol	5 mg
Sodium	69 mg
Potassium	375 mg
Total Carbohydrate	58 g
Dietary Fiber	5 g
Sugars	42 g
Protein	6 g
Calcium 13% • Magnesium 11%	

Grown-Up Berry Parfait
Serves 2

¼ cup sliced strawberries

¼ cup blueberries

¼ cup raspberries

4 tablespoons Grand Marnier liqueur

1 teaspoon grated lemon zest

2 cups low-fat plain Greek yogurt

½ teaspoon vanilla extract

¼ cup toasted unsalted chopped pecans

In a medium bowl, combine the berries, Grand Marnier, and lemon zest, and let sit for about 20 minutes, stirring occasionally. In a large bowl, mix the yogurt and vanilla together. In two tall glasses, create parfaits by alternating layers of the yogurt mixture and the berry mixture. Top with pecans.

Nutrition Facts *(amount per serving)*	
Calories	310
Total Fat	11 g
Saturated Fat	0.9 g
Polyunsaturated Fat	3 g
Monounsaturated Fat	6 g
Cholesterol	0 mg
Sodium	81 mg
Potassium	121 mg
Total Carbohydrate	22 g
Dietary Fiber	3 g
Sugars	18 g
Protein	22 g
Calcium 28% • Magnesium 11%	

Healthy Mini Cheesecakes with Vanilla Wafer Almond Crust

Serves 6 (Makes 12 cakes)

CRUST

3½ ounces vanilla wafers (½ small box)

½ cup toasted, slivered almonds

½ teaspoon ground cinnamon

¼ cup flaxseeds

4 tablespoons extra virgin olive oil

CHEESECAKE BATTER

1 cup whole milk ricotta cheese

2 cups low-fat plain Greek yogurt

1 tablespoon maple syrup

Grated zest of ½ lime

Grated zest of ½ lemon

Juice of ½ lemon

1 teaspoon vanilla extract

1 egg, beaten

¼ cup flour

Preheat the oven to 350°F.

To make the crust, mix the wafers, almonds, cinnamon, and flaxseeds in a food processor until the mixture looks like flour. Drizzle in oil until the mixture holds together. Grease a 12-cup muffin tin with olive oil spray. Divide the mixture among the cups, and mold the crust inside each with your fingers, making the crust go all the way up the sides. Bake 8 to 10 minutes, or until the crusts darken and you can smell them. Remove from the oven, and let cool completely.

To make the batter, in a large bowl whisk together all the ingredients except the egg and flour until there are no lumps.

Add the beaten egg to the batter, and mix thoroughly. Add the flour, mixing with a spatula until incorporated.

Pour the batter into the cooled crusts, return to the 350°F oven, and bake for an additional 15 to 20 minutes, or until you shake the pan and the filling doesn't jiggle. Remove from the oven, and cool completely.

Serving suggestion: If crumbs get stuck to the bottom of the pan when you're removing the mini cheesecakes, use the crumbs to top the cheesecakes. Other toppings include fresh blueberries, blackberries, and raspberries.

Nutrition Facts *(amount per serving)*	
Calories	367
Total Fat	23 g
Saturated Fat	5 g
Polyunsaturated Fat	5 g
Monounsaturated Fat	12 g
Cholesterol	21 mg
Sodium	134 mg
Potassium	226 mg
Total Carbohydrate	25 g
Dietary Fiber	5 g
Sugars	10 g
Protein	16 g
Calcium 25% • Magnesium 10%	

Delicious Oatmeal Cookies

Makes 36 cookies; 1 cookie per serving

½ cup unsalted butter, at room temperature

¾ cup firmly packed brown sugar

2 large eggs

1 teaspoon vanilla extract

1 cup whole wheat flour

½ cup brown rice flour

3 tablespoons flaxseeds

1 teaspoon baking soda

½ teaspoon ground cinnamon

⅛ teaspoon ground ginger

⅛ teaspoon ground nutmeg

3 cups old-fashioned oats

1 cup raisins

1 cup toasted chopped walnuts

Preheat the oven to 350°F.

In a large bowl, beat the butter and sugar with an electric mixer on medium speed until creamy. Add the eggs and vanilla, and beat well. In a separate large bowl, combine the flours, flaxseeds, baking soda, cinnamon, ginger, and nutmeg. Add the dry mixture in three batches to the wet mixture, incorporating evenly after each batch. Add the oats, raisins, and walnuts, and mix by hand with a spatula until evenly incorporated.

Drop the dough by rounded tablespoonful onto ungreased cookie sheets. Be careful not to overcrowd them.

Bake 8 to 10 minutes, or until light golden brown. Cool 1 minute on the cookie sheets, and then transfer to a wire rack. Repeat process for the second batch of cookies. Cool completely, and store tightly covered.

Nutrition Facts *(amount per serving)*	
Calories	130
Total Fat	6 g
Saturated Fat	2 g
Polyunsaturated Fat	2 g
Monounsaturated Fat	2 g
Cholesterol	17 mg
Sodium	43 mg
Potassium	140 mg
Total Carbohydrate	23 g
Dietary Fiber	3 g
Sugars	9 g
Protein	3 g
Calcium 2% • Magnesium 8%	

Vegan Date Nut Loaf
Serves 10

1 cup chopped pitted dates

1 cup coarsely chopped unsalted pecans

1½ teaspoons baking soda

⅛ teaspoon salt

3 tablespoons extra virgin olive oil

¾ cup boiling water

1½ medium ripe bananas, mashed

¼ cup firmly packed brown sugar

1 teaspoon vanilla extract

½ teaspoon ground cinnamon

⅛ teaspoon ground nutmeg

⅛ teaspoon ground ginger

1½ cups whole wheat flour

Preheat the oven to 350°F. Spray an 8- by 4-inch loaf pan with olive oil spray.

In a large bowl, combine the dates, pecans, baking soda, salt, and oil. Pour the boiling water over the mixture, and stir to incorporate. Let stand for 15 minutes.

In a separate large bowl, mash the bananas with a fork, and add the sugar, vanilla, cinnamon, nutmeg, and ginger. Stir with a spoon. Add the flour, and stir. Add the date mixture, folding in the ingredients with a spatula until the batter is well blended. Be careful not to overstir once all ingredients are incorporated. Spoon the mixture into the loaf pan, and bake for 35 to 45 minutes, or until an inserted toothpick comes out clean. Check the loaf after 35 minutes. The bread will continue to bake after it is removed from the oven, so be careful not to overbake. Once the loaf has cooled slightly, slide a knife around the edges of the pan, and turn the loaf onto a rack to cool completely. Cut into 10 slices.

Nutrition Facts *(amount per serving)*	
Calories	268
Total Fat	13 g
Saturated Fat	2 g
Polyunsaturated Fat	3 g
Monounsaturated Fat	8 g
Cholesterol	0 mg
Sodium	22 mg
Potassium	256 mg
Total Carbohydrate	40 g
Dietary Fiber	5 g
Sugars	21 g
Protein	4 g
Calcium 2% • Magnesium 6%	

Zucchini Carrot Bread
Serves 10

1 cup whole wheat flour

½ cup all-purpose flour

⅛ teaspoon sea salt

½ teaspoon baking powder

½ teaspoon baking soda

½ teaspoon ground ginger

1½ teaspoons ground cinnamon

2 eggs

¼ cup extra virgin olive oil

¼ cup unsweetened applesauce

½ cup firmly packed brown sugar

1 teaspoon vanilla extract

1½ cups shredded zucchini

½ cup shredded carrots

½ cup toasted chopped walnuts

Preheat the oven to 325°F. Spray an 8- by 4-inch pan with olive oil spray.

In a medium bowl, sift together the flours, salt, baking powder, baking soda, ginger, and cinnamon. In a separate large bowl, beat the eggs, oil, applesauce, sugar, and vanilla with an electric mixer. Add the sifted ingredients to the wet ingredients, and beat well until there are no more dry spots in the batter, about 30 seconds. Stir in the zucchini (do not drain or wring out), carrots, and nuts with a spatula until well combined. Pour the batter into the prepared pan.

Bake for 40 to 50 minutes, or until an inserted toothpick comes out clean. Check the loaf after 40 minutes. Cool in the pan on a rack for 20 minutes. Remove from the pan, and cool completely. Cut into 10 slices.

Nutrition Facts *(amount per serving)*	
Calories	216
Total Fat	11 g
Saturated Fat	2 g
Polyunsaturated Fat	4 g
Monounsaturated Fat	5 g
Cholesterol	37 mg
Sodium	111 mg
Potassium	181 mg
Total Carbohydrate	31 g
Dietary Fiber	3 g
Sugars	16 g
Protein	5 g
Calcium 4% • Magnesium 5%	

Mini Banana Vegan Muffins
Serves 6 (Makes 12 mini muffins)

½ cup whole wheat flour

¼ cup all-purpose flour

½ teaspoon baking soda

½ teaspoon baking powder

½ teaspoon ground cinnamon

⅛ teaspoon salt

2 medium ripe bananas

¼ cup firmly packed brown sugar

⅛ cup unsweetened applesauce

⅛ teaspoon vanilla extract

1½ tablespoons extra virgin olive oil

¼ cup toasted chopped walnuts

Preheat the oven to 375°F. Spray a mini muffin pan with olive oil spray.

In a large bowl, sift together the flours, baking soda, baking powder, cinnamon, and salt. In a separate large bowl, mash the bananas, and add the brown sugar, applesauce, vanilla, and oil. Stir the flour mixture into the banana mixture just until moistened. Do not overstir the batter. Fold in the walnuts.

Using a teaspoon, spoon the batter into the prepared muffin cups. Bake for 15 to 18 minutes, or until a toothpick inserted into center of a muffin comes out clean. Do not overbake.

Nutrition Facts (amount per serving)	
Calories	188
Total Fat	7 g
Saturated Fat	0.9 g
Polyunsaturated Fat	3 g
Monounsaturated Fat	3 g
Cholesterol	0 mg
Sodium	150 mg
Potassium	221 mg
Total Carbohydrate	34 g
Dietary Fiber	3 g
Sugars	18 g
Protein	3 g
Calcium 4% • Magnesium 5%	

Zucchini Muffins
Serves 12 (Makes 12 muffins)

⅔ cup extra virgin olive oil

2 large eggs

½ cup firmly packed brown sugar

¼ cup honey

1 teaspoon vanilla extract

1 cup all-purpose flour

1 cup whole wheat flour

½ teaspoon baking soda

½ teaspoon baking powder

⅛ teaspoon sea salt

2 teaspoons ground cinnamon

2½ cups shredded zucchini

¼ cup old-fashioned oats

½ cup toasted chopped walnuts

¼ cup flaxseeds

Preheat the oven to 375°F. Spray the muffin tin with olive oil spray.

In a large bowl, whisk the oil with the eggs, sugar, honey, and vanilla until slightly creamy. In a separate large bowl, sift the flours, baking soda, baking powder, salt, and cinnamon. Add the sifted ingredients to the wet ingredients, stirring with a spatula until blended. Fold in the shredded zucchini, oats, walnuts, and flaxseeds. Stir with a spatula until there are no more dry spots in the batter. Scoop into the muffin cups, sprinkle with cinnamon, and bake for 20 to 22 minutes, or until a toothpick inserted comes out clean.

COOKING TIPS

• Shredded zucchini produces a lot of moisture, so sometimes it's necessary to place shredded zucchini between paper towels and wring out extra liquid.

• Using a spatula instead of an electric mixer helps to avoid overmixing the batter, which can make it tough.

Nutrition Facts (amount per serving)	
Calories	362
Total Fat	25 g
Saturated Fat	3 g
Polyunsaturated Fat	6 g
Monounsaturated Fat	15 g
Cholesterol	31 mg
Sodium	91 mg
Potassium	221 mg
Total Carbohydrate	39 g
Dietary Fiber	4 g
Sugars	19 g
Protein	5 g
Calcium 5% • Magnesium 6%	

Berry Cobbler
Serves 6

2 tablespoons cornstarch

¼ teaspoon ground cinnamon

¼ cup cold water

1 (16-ounce) package frozen mixed berries

2 tablespoons brown sugar

1 tablespoon grated lemon zest

CRUMBLE TOPPING

½ cup whole wheat flour

¼ cup old-fashioned oats

1½ teaspoons flaxseeds

⅛ cup toasted chopped walnuts

¼ teaspoon ground nutmeg

5 tablespoons cold, unsalted butter

Preheat the oven to 375°F. In a large saucepan, combine the cornstarch, cinnamon, and water, and bring to a boil. Continue to boil, and stir until thick, about 2 minutes. Remove from the heat, and add the berries, sugar, and lemon zest. Stir to coat the berries.

To make the topping, combine the flour, oats, flaxseeds, walnuts, nutmeg, and cold butter in a medium bowl. Scrunch with your fingers until the mixture becomes crumbly and holds together.

Coat an 8-inch pie pan or round baking dish with olive oil spray, and pour in the berry mixture. Top the berries with the crumble topping, and bake for 20 to 25 minutes, or until the berries are bubbling and the topping is crunchy to the touch and cooked through.

Nutrition Facts (amount per serving)	
Calories	204
Total Fat	13 g
Saturated Fat	6 g
Polyunsaturated Fat	3 g
Monounsaturated Fat	3 g
Cholesterol	26 mg
Sodium	4 mg
Potassium	94 mg
Total Carbohydrate	24 g
Dietary Fiber	3 g
Sugars	0.5 g
Protein	8 g
Calcium 2% • Magnesium 5%	

Section Four

THE 28-DAY
DASH
MEAL PLAN

For a true DASH experience, follow this meal plan for the next month. It maps out breakfast, lunch, snack, dinner, and dessert every day, utilizing Chef Anna's recipes and following DASH guidelines.

The plan is based on 2,000 calories per day, and a modification for 1,200 calories per day is offered in italicized parentheses.

Although water isn't listed as part of each meal, drinking lots of water is always recommended. A good formula for calculating minimum water intake is to divide your weight in half and drink that many ounces of water each day. For example, a 130-pound woman should drink 65 ounces of water each day (at least eight 8-ounce glasses).

DAY 1

BREAKFAST
Blueberry Green Smoothie, page 39
2 slices 100% whole wheat toast *(1 slice)* with 2 tablespoons peanut butter *(1 tablespoon)*

LUNCH
1 serving Insalata di Farro *(¾ serving)*, page 82
8 ounces nonfat milk
1 medium orange *(small)*

SNACK
1 cup cherries *(½ cup)*
20 almonds *(10 almonds)*

DINNER

>1 serving Healthy Italian Pasta Salad *(½ serving)*, page 88
>
>5 ounces grilled or baked boneless, skinless chicken breast *(3 ounces)*
>
>1 cup frozen grapes *(½ cup)*

DAY 2

BREAKFAST

>1 Egg Muffin, page 73
>
>½ grapefruit
>
>Coffee with 4 ounces nonfat milk, or green tea with lemon

LUNCH

>1 serving Broccoli Soup, page 174, topped with grated Parmesan cheese *(no cheese)*
>
>¼ cup hummus *(2 tablespoons)* with baby carrots and sliced bell pepper
>
>1 cup strawberries

SNACK

>8 ounces nonfat plain Greek yogurt *(4 ounces)* with ½ cup blueberries

DINNER

>4 Turkey Meatballs in Marinara Sauce *(3 meatballs)*, page 134
>
>1 cup steamed spinach with garlic and 1 teaspoon extra virgin olive oil
>
>1 slice 100% whole wheat bread
>
>2 slices fresh pineapple *(1 slice)*
>
>6–8 ounces sparkling water

DAY 3

BREAKFAST

2 slices Toast with Almond Butter and Banana *(1 slice)*, page 53

8 ounces nonfat milk, or coffee with up to 8 ounces nonfat milk

LUNCH

2 servings Mexican Summer Salad *(1½ cups)*, page 94

½ sliced avocado

20 almonds *(10 almonds)*

1 medium peach *(small)*

SNACK

1 medium apple, sliced, with 2 tablespoons peanut butter or almond butter *(1 tablespoon)*

DINNER

1 serving Stuffed Bell Pepper *(½ serving)*, page 142

1 cup steamed broccoli

1 serving Grown-Up Berry Parfait, page 235 *(1 serving Berry Sundae, page 215)*

DAY 4

BREAKFAST

1 serving Berries Deluxe Oatmeal, page 57

LUNCH

1 serving Grilled Romaine Salad with 1 tablespoon Garlicky Balsamic Vinaigrette, page 95

4 ounces baked boneless, skinless chicken breast *(2 ounces)*

½ 100% whole wheat pita bread

1 banana *(½ banana)*

SNACK

½ cup nonfat cottage cheese with ½ cup sliced cucumbers and cherry tomatoes

1 medium orange *(small)*

DINNER

1 serving Sesame Salmon Fillets *(½ serving)*, page 144

1 cup baked sweet potato *(½ cup)*

1 cup steamed spinach

1 Grilled Peach with Ricotta Stuffing and Balsamic Glaze *(½ grilled peach with cinnamon, no ricotta or glaze)*, page 217

DAY 5

BREAKFAST

1 serving Banana Almond Smoothie, page 43

2 slices 100% whole wheat bread *(1 slice)*

2 ounces goat cheese *(1 ounce)*

LUNCH

1 serving Tuna Salad *(½ serving)*, page 120, with 1½ cups spinach

½ sliced avocado *(¼ avocado)*

½ cup cherry tomatoes

1 cup mixed berries

SNACK

2 multigrain rice cakes *(1 rice cake)*

¼ cup hummus *(2 tablespoons)*

DINNER

1 serving Thai Curried Vegetables, page 150

1 cup brown rice *(½ cup)*

½ cup strawberries with 1 tablespoon homemade Whipped Cream *(no whipped cream)*, page 228

DAY 6

BREAKFAST
  1 serving Warm Quinoa with Berries, page 62
  1 tablespoon sliced almonds *(1 teaspoon)*
  Coffee with 8 ounces nonfat milk, or tea

LUNCH
  1 Chicken Fajita Wrap *(½ wrap)*, page 110
  ¼ cup Tropical Salsa, page 179
  1 medium orange *(small)*

SNACK
  2 ounces mozzarella cheese *(1 ounce)*
  ½ cup grapes *(¼ cup)*

DINNER
  2 Fish Tacos *(1 taco)*, page 148
  1 cup Anna's Black Beans *(½ cup)*, page 164
  ½ cup Tropical Salsa *(¼ cup)*, page 179
  2 slices Grilled Pineapple *(1 slice)*, page 218

DAY 7

BREAKFAST
  1 serving Tropical Smoothie, page 44
  1 100% whole wheat English muffin *(½ muffin)*
  with 2 tablespoons peanut butter or almond butter
  (1 tablespoon)

LUNCH
  1 serving Italian Veggie Pita Sandwich, page 114, with
  4 ounces grilled or baked boneless, skinless chicken
  breast *(2 ounces)*
  8 ounces nonfat milk *(4 ounces)*
  ½ cup grapes

SNACK

¼ cup hummus *(2 tablespoons)* with sliced bell pepper and cucumber

DINNER

2 Grilled Chicken Skewers Marinated in Ginger-Apricot Sauce *(1 skewer)*, page 128

1 cup brown rice *(½ cup)*

1 cup Roasted Cauliflower, page 206

1 Brie-Stuffed Apple *(no brie)*, page 222

DAY 8

BREAKFAST

1 serving Fruity Yogurt Parfait, page 63

1 tablespoon almonds *(1 teaspoon)*

Coffee with 4 ounces nonfat milk *(2 ounces)*

LUNCH

1 serving Kale Vegetable Soup, page 118

8 ounces nonfat milk

1 toasted cheese sandwich with reduced-fat mozzarella cheese on 1 slice 100% whole wheat bread *(no sandwich)*

SNACK

¼ cup Hummus Dip with Curried Pita Chips *(2 tablespoons)*, page 190

½ cup grapes *(¼ cup)*

DINNER

2 slices Mexican Pizza *(1 slice)*, page 160

1 serving Beet and Heirloom Tomato Salad *(½ serving)*, page 99

1 cup Macerated Strawberries with Homemade Whipped Cream *(no whipped cream)*, page 228

DAY 9

BREAKFAST

1 Open-Faced Breakfast Sandwich *(no cheese)*, page 65

8 ounces nonfat milk, or coffee with up to 8 ounces nonfat milk

1 cup mixed berries

LUNCH

1 serving Healthy Cobb Salad with 1 tablespoon Basic Vinaigrette, page 96

1 100% whole wheat pita bread *(no pita bread)*

1 medium apple *(small)*

SNACK

1 cup air-popped popcorn with 1 teaspoon butter *(no butter)*

1 medium orange *(small)*

DINNER

1 Grilled Portobello Burger with Caramelized Onions and Pesto *(light pesto)*, page 153

1 serving Grilled Sweet Potato Steak Fries *(½ serving)*, page 194

1 serving Banana Chocolate Dessert Smoothie *(½ serving)*, page 233

DAY 10

BREAKFAST

1 serving Mediterranean Scramble *(2 egg whites only)*, page 72

Coffee with up to 8 ounces nonfat milk

1 slice 100% whole wheat bread *(no bread)*

½ cup grapes

LUNCH
1 serving Asian Quinoa Salad *(½ serving)*, page 84

½ cup baby carrots

1 medium peach *(small)*

SNACK
20 almonds *(10 almonds)*

1 banana

DINNER
1 serving Orange Chicken *(½ serving)* and 1 cup Brown Rice *(½ cup)*, page 126

1 cup steamed spinach

1 serving Berry Cobbler, page 248 *(½ cup mixed berries)*

DAY 11

BREAKFAST
1 serving English Muffin with Berries, page 54

1 hard-boiled egg

Coffee with up to 8 ounces nonfat milk

LUNCH
1 serving Pomegranate Salad, page 98, with 2 tablespoons Garlicky Balsamic Vinaigrette *(1 tablespoon)*, page 93

1 100% whole wheat pita bread *(½ pita bread)*

1 medium peach *(small)*

SNACK
¼ cup Hummus Dip *(2 tablespoons)*, page 190, with baby carrots and sliced bell pepper

DINNER

1 serving Baked Sunflower Seed–Crusted Turkey Cutlets *(½ serving)*, page 132

1½ cups roasted mixed vegetables, such as broccoli, green beans, and asparagus

1 medium baked sweet potato *(½ medium)* with 1 tablespoon butter *(no butter)*

1 serving Mexican Fruit Salad *(½ serving)*, page 230

DAY 12

BREAKFAST

1 serving Protein Bowl *(½ serving)*, page 56

2 slices 100% whole wheat toast *(1 slice)* with 2 tablespoons 100% fruit jam *(1 tablespoon)*

Green tea

LUNCH

1 serving Greek Salad with 1 tablespoon Lemon Vinaigrette, page 100, with 4 ounces grilled or baked boneless, skinless chicken breast *(2 ounces)*

1 medium apple *(small)*

20 almonds *(10 almonds)*

SNACK

8 ounces nonfat plain yogurt *(4 ounces)*

1 cup mixed berries

DINNER

1 serving Thai Curried Vegetables, page 150, with 3 ounces baked or grilled boneless, skinless chicken breast *(2 ounces)*

1 cup brown rice *(½ cup)*

1 Mini Banana Split *(½ mini split)*, page 234

DAY 13

BREAKFAST

1 serving Wake Up Call! smoothie, page 41

1 hard-boiled egg

1 slice 100% whole wheat toast

LUNCH

2 Beef Tacos *(1 taco)*, page 106

¼ cup Grandma's Guacamole *(2½ tablespoons)*, page 180

1 medium orange *(small)*

SNACK

1 100% whole wheat English muffin *(½ muffin)*
with 2 tablespoons peanut butter or almond butter
(1 tablespoon) and 1 sliced banana *(½ banana)*

DINNER

1 serving Spice-Rubbed Salmon *(½ serving)*, page 145

1½ cups Sautéed Vegetables, page 207

1 cup Cilantro-Lime Brown Rice *(½ cup)*, page 209

1 cup frozen grapes

DAY 14

BREAKFAST

2 Egg Muffins, page 73

1 100% whole wheat English muffin *(½ muffin)* with
2 tablespoons goat cheese *(2 teaspoons)*

½ grapefruit

LUNCH

1 serving Grilled Chicken with Black Bean Salsa *(½ serving)*, page 105

1½ cups green salad with 1 tablespoon Garlicky
Balsamic Vinaigrette, page 93

2 corn tortillas *(1 tortilla)*

1 cup grapes

SNACK

¼ cup raw unsalted nuts *(2 tablespoons)*

1 medium apple *(small)*

DINNER

1 serving Turkey Chili, page 115

1 serving Beet and Heirloom Tomato Salad, page 99

1 100% whole wheat pita bread *(½ pita bread)*

1 serving Berry Cobbler, page 248 *(1 cup mixed berries)*

DAY 15

BREAKFAST

1 serving Berry Banana Green Smoothie, page 45

Coffee with up to 8 ounces nonfat milk *(4 ounces)*

1 slice 100% whole wheat toast with 1 tablespoon 100% fruit raspberry jam *(no toast, no jam)*

LUNCH

1 serving Tuna Salad, page 120, topped with ½ sliced avocado *(¼ avocado)*

½ 100% whole wheat pita bread *(no pita)*

1 medium orange *(small)*

SNACK

1 medium, sliced apple *(small)*

2 tablespoons peanut butter *(1 tablespoon)*

DINNER

1 serving Turkey Chili *(½ serving)*, page 115, with 2 tablespoons shredded cheddar cheese *(1 tablespoon)*

Small spinach salad with assorted veggies, like tomato, cucumber, carrot, bell pepper, and 2 tablespoons Basic Vinaigrette *(1 tablespoon)*, page 90

1 serving Berry Sundae, page 215

DAY 16

BREAKFAST

1 Healthy "Lox" English Muffin *(½ muffin)*, page 55

½ grapefruit

Coffee with up to 8 ounces nonfat milk *(4 ounces)*

LUNCH

1 serving Roasted Butternut Squash Soup *(½ serving)*, page 172

½ cup sliced strawberries

1 cup baby carrots

SNACK

8 ounces nonfat plain yogurt *(6 ounces)*

½ cup blueberries

¼ cup almonds *(2 tablespoons)*

DINNER

2 Fish Tacos *(1 taco)*, page 148

½ cup Tropical Salsa *(¼ cup)*, page 179

1 cup mixed berries with 2 tablespoons homemade Whipped Cream *(no whipped cream)*, page 228

DAY 17

BREAKFAST

2 slices Healthy French Toast *(1 slice)*, page 80, with 2 tablespoons real maple syrup *(1 tablespoon)*

½ cup mixed berries

8 ounces nonfat milk *(4 ounces)*

LUNCH

1 serving Italian Veggie Pita Sandwich, page 114

2 tablespoons hummus *(1 tablespoon)* with 1 cup baby carrots

1 medium peach *(small)*

SNACK

1 banana

¼ cup raw unsalted cashews *(2 tablespoons)*

DINNER

1 serving Turkey Roulade with Cider Sauce *(½ serving)*, page 139

1 medium baked sweet potato *(½ sweet potato)*

1 cup steamed spinach

1 Brie-Stuffed Apple *(no brie)*, page 222

DAY 18

BREAKFAST

1 serving Green Avocado Smoothie, page 47

Green tea

½ 100% whole wheat English muffin with 2 tablespoons peanut butter *(1 tablespoon)*

LUNCH

1 Chicken Fajita Wrap *(½ wrap)*, page 110

½ cup Grandma's Guacamole *(¼ cup)*, page 180, with 1 cup baby carrots

1 medium orange *(small)*

SNACK

½ cup sliced strawberries

½ cup sliced banana

DINNER

1 serving Healthier Mac 'n' Cheese, page 162

1 serving Greek Salad with 2 tablespoons Lemon Vinaigrette *(1 tablespoon)*, page 100

½ 100% whole wheat pita bread *(no pita)*

1 serving Banana Chocolate Dessert Smoothie *(½ serving)*, page 233

DAY 19

BREAKFAST

Veggie Omelet, page 74

½ cup mixed berries

Coffee with up to 8 ounces nonfat milk *(4 ounces)*

LUNCH

2 servings Chicken Pasta Salad *(1 serving)*, page 86

1 cup sliced carrot, bell pepper, and cucumber with 2 tablespoons Basic Vinaigrette *(1 tablespoon)*, page 90

1 medium pear *(small)*

SNACK

4 ounces nonfat cottage cheese

¼ cup raw unsalted cashews *(2 tablespoons)*

1 medium sliced apple *(small)*

DINNER

1 serving Sesame Salmon Fillets *(½ serving)*, page 144

1 serving Grilled Asparagus, page 196

1 cup brown rice *(½ cup)*

1 serving Grown-Up Berry Parfait *(½ serving)*, page 235

DAY 20

BREAKFAST

1 serving Melon Mélange smoothie, page 48

1 serving Anna's Homemade Granola *(½ serving)*, page 60

LUNCH

1 serving Grilled Romaine Salad with 1 tablespoon Garlicky Balsamic Vinaigrette, page 95, and 3 ounces grilled boneless, skinless chicken breast *(2 ounces)*

1 cup grapes

SNACK

1 cup air-popped popcorn

½ cup baby carrots

½ sliced medium apple

DINNER

1 serving Turkey Meat Loaf, page 136

1 medium mashed sweet potato *(small)* with 1 teaspoon butter *(no butter)*

1 serving Greek Salad with 1 tablespoon Lemon Vinaigrette, page 100

1 cup mixed berries

DAY 21

BREAKFAST

1 serving Energy Oatmeal, page 59

8 ounces nonfat milk *(4 ounces)*

½ grapefruit

LUNCH

1 serving Healthy Cobb Salad with 1 tablespoon Basic Vinaigrette, page 96

½ 100% whole wheat pita bread *(no pita)*

1 cup grapes

SNACK

¼ cup hummus with 1 cup cherry tomatoes, sliced bell pepper, and cucumber

2 tablespoons hazelnuts *(1 tablespoon)*

DINNER

2 slices Mexican Pizza *(1 slice)*, page 160, with 5 ounces grilled or baked boneless, skinless chicken breast *(3 ounces)*

2 servings Greek Salad with 2 tablespoons Lemon Vinaigrette *(1 tablespoon)*, page 100

1 Grilled Peach with Ricotta Stuffing and Balsamic Glaze *(½ grilled peach with cinnamon, no ricotta or glaze)*, page 217

DAY 22

BREAKFAST

2 Whole Grain Pancakes *(1 pancake)*, page 78, with 2 tablespoons real maple syrup *(1 tablespoon)*

Coffee with up to 8 ounces nonfat milk *(4 ounces)*

½ cup sliced strawberries

LUNCH

1 serving Italian-Style Tuna Salad *(¾ serving)*, page 121 with 1½ cups spinach

1 medium kiwifruit

SNACK

1 serving Blueberry Green Smoothie, page 39

DINNER

1 serving Chicken Fajitas (no avocado sauce), page 130, with 3 corn tortillas *(2 tortillas)*

¼ cup Grandma's Guacamole *(2 tablespoons)*, page 180

½ cup Anna's Black Beans *(¼ cup)*, page 164

1 cup Mexican Fruit Salad *(½ cup)*, page 230

DAY 23

BREAKFAST

1 serving Berry Banana Green Smoothie, page 45

½ 100% whole wheat English muffin with 1 tablespoon goat cheese *(no muffin, no cheese)*

Coffee with up to 8 ounces nonfat milk *(4 ounces)*

LUNCH

6 ounces Grilled Chicken with Black Bean Salsa *(3 ounces)*, page 105

Tomato and cucumber salad with 2 tablespoons Basic Vinaigrette *(1 tablespoon)*, page 90

1 medium peach *(small)*

SNACK

1 medium banana with 2 tablespoons peanut butter *(1 tablespoon)*

DINNER

Grilled Portobello Burger with Caramelized Onions and Pesto, page 153

1 serving Grilled Sweet Potato Steak Fries *(½ serving)*, page 194

¾ cup Macerated Strawberries with Homemade Whipped Cream *(no whipped cream)*, page 228

DAY 24

BREAKFAST

1 serving Protein Bowl, page 56

½ grapefruit

Green tea

LUNCH

2 cups Anna's Black Beans, page 164, with 1 tablespoon sour cream *(no sour cream)*

Small salad with 1 cup mixed greens, cherry tomatoes, and sliced cucumber

1 medium orange

SNACK

¼ cup Grandma's Guacamole *(2 tablespoons)*, page 180, with 1 cup baby carrots and sliced bell pepper

DINNER

1 serving Pan-Steamed Orange Roughy *(½ serving)*, page 146

1 cup steamed spinach

6 small roasted red potatoes *(3 small potatoes)*

1 serving Mini Banana Split, page 234 *(small banana with 1 tablespoon chocolate)*

DAY 25

BREAKFAST

1 serving Apples and Cinnamon Oatmeal, page 57

1 hard-boiled egg

8 ounces nonfat milk

LUNCH

1 serving Curried Chicken Salad Pita Sandwich *(½ serving)*, page 108

1 cup baby carrots and sliced bell peppers

1 cup cherries

SNACK

8 ounces nonfat plain yogurt *(6 ounces)*

1 cup mixed berries

20 almonds *(10 almonds)*

DINNER

2 servings Roasted Butternut Squash Soup *(1 serving)*, page 172, topped with 1 tablespoon low-fat yogurt *(no yogurt)*

1 serving Brussels Sprouts Casserole *(no pancetta)*, page 200

1 serving Pomegranate Salad, page 98, with 2 tablespoons dressing *(1 tablespoon)*

1 Delicious Oatmeal Cookie *(no cookie)*, page 238

DAY 26

BREAKFAST

1 serving Warm Quinoa with Berries *(no pecans)*, page 62

8 ounces nonfat milk

LUNCH

1 serving Insalata di Farro, page 82, with 4 ounces grilled or baked boneless, skinless chicken breast *(2 ounces)*

1 medium orange *(small)*

SNACK

1 piece light string cheese

1 cup grapes *(¾ cup)*

DINNER

4 Turkey Meatballs in Marinara Sauce *(3 meatballs)*, page 134

1 serving Greek Salad with 1 tablespoon Lemon Vinaigrette, page 100

1 serving Brandied Peaches and Apples with Caramel Pecans, page 226 *(1 cup sliced peaches and apples)*

DAY 27

BREAKFAST

1 serving Peach Green Smoothie, page 46

½ 100% whole wheat English muffin with 2 tablespoons peanut butter *(no English muffin, no peanut butter)*

Coffee with up to 8 ounces nonfat milk *(4 ounces)*

LUNCH

½ cup black beans with 2 corn tortillas and 2 tablespoons cheddar cheese, ¼ cup salsa, ½ sliced avocado *(no cheese, ¼ avocado)*

Small spinach salad with 1 cup diced bell pepper, cucumber, and grape tomatoes

2 tablespoons Basic Vinaigrette *(1 tablespoon)*, page 90

SNACK

20 hazelnuts *(10 hazelnuts)*

8 ounces nonfat plain yogurt *(4 ounces)*

½ cup sliced strawberries

DINNER

1 serving Baked Sunflower Seed–Crusted Turkey Cutlets *(½ serving)*, page 132

1 serving Brussels Sprouts Casserole *(no pancetta)*, page 200

1 medium baked sweet potato *(½ sweet potato)*

1 serving Berry Cobbler, page 248 *(½ cup blueberries)*

DAY 28

BREAKFAST

1 serving Pumpkin Pie Smoothie, page 50, with 1 tablespoon peanut butter, either mixed in or separate

1 slice 100% whole wheat bread with 1 tablespoon goat cheese *(no bread, no cheese)*

Coffee with up to 8 ounces nonfat milk *(4 ounces)*

LUNCH

1 serving Mom's Bean Soup *(no cheese)*, page 176

½ cup cherry tomatoes

½ cup baby carrots

1 medium apple *(small)*

SNACK

8 ounces nonfat plain yogurt

1 medium banana

20 almonds *(10 almonds)*

DINNER

6 ounces baked boneless, skinless chicken breast *(3 ounces)*

1 serving Caprese Salad with Balsamic Glaze *(½ serving)*, page 101

4 small roasted red potatoes *(2 small potatoes)*

2 Healthy Mini Cheesecakes with Vanilla Wafer Almond Crust *(1 mini cheesecake)*, page 236

Resources

Appel, L. J., M. W. Brands, S. R. Daniels, N. Karanja, P. J. Elmer, and F. M. Sacks. "Dietary Approaches to Prevent and Treat Hypertension: a Scientific Statement from the American Heart Association." *Hypertension* 2006 February; 47(2):296-308.

Blumenthal, J. A., M. A. Babyak, A. Hinderliter, L. L. Watkins, L. Craighead, P. H. Lin, C. Caccia, J. Johnson, R. Waugh, A. Sherwood. "Effects of the DASH Diet Alone and in Combination with Exercise and Weight Loss on Blood Pressure and Cardiovascular Biomarkers in Men and Women with High Blood Pressure: The ENCORE Study." *Arch Intern Med* January 25, 2010; 170(2):126-35.

de Koning L., S. E. Chiuve, T. T. Fung, W. C. Willett, E. B. Rimm, and F. B. Hu. "Diet-Quality Scores and the Risk of Type 2 Diabetes in Men." *Diabetes Care.* 2011 May; 34(5):1150-6.

Elmer P. J., E. Obarzanek, W. M. Vollmer, et al. "Effects of Comprehensive Lifestyle Modification on Diet, Weight, Physical Fitness, and Blood Pressure Control: 18-Month Results of a Randomized Trial." *Ann Intern Med* 2006 April 4; 144(7):485-95.

Karanja, N., T. P. Erlinger, L. Pao-Hwa, E. R. Miller ER, III, and G. A. Bray. "The DASH Diet for High Blood Pressure:

From Clinical Trial to Dinner Table." *Cleve Clin J Med* 2004 September; 71(9):745-53.

Levitan, E. B., A. Wolk, and M.A. Mittleman. "Consistency with the DASH Diet and Incidence of Heart Failure." *Arch Intern Med* 2009; 169(9):851-857.

Moore, Thomas, MD, and Laura Svetky, MD, et al. *The DASH Diet for Hypertension*. New York: Simon & Schuster, 2001.

Obarzanek E., Moore T. J. Using Feeding Studies to Test the Efficacy of Dietary Interventions: Lessons from the Dietary Approaches to Stop Hypertension Trial. *J Am Diet Assoc* 99 (Suppl): S9-S11, 1999.

Sacks, F. M., L. P. Svetkey, W. M. Vollmer, et al. "Effects on Blood Pressure of Reduced Dietary Sodium and the Dietary Approaches to Stop Hypertension (DASH) Diet." *N Engl J Med* 2001 January 4; 344:3-10.

Taylor, E. N., T. T. Fung, and G. C. Curhan. "DASH-Style Diet Associates with Reduced Risk for Kidney Stones." *J Am Soc Neph* October 20:2253-59.

U.S. Department of Health and Human Services. "Your Guide to Lowering Your Blood Pressure with DASH" (PDF). April 2006. Retrieved 2011-12-28.

Index

Anna's Black Beans, 164–65

Anna's Homemade Granola, 60–61

Apples and Cinnamon Oatmeal, 57

Arugula Smoothie, 51

Asian Quinoa Salad, 84–85

Asian-Style Lettuce Wraps with Peanut Sauce, 112–13

Baked Sunflower Seed–Crusted Turkey Cutlets, 132–33

Balsamic Glaze, 89

Banana Almond Smoothie, 43

Banana Almond Yogurt, 64

Banana Chocolate Dessert Smoothie, 233

Basic Vinaigrette, 90

Beef Tacos, 106–107

Beet and Heirloom Tomato Salad, 99

Berries Deluxe Oatmeal, 57

Berry Banana Green Smoothie, 45

Berry Cobbler, 248–49

Berry Sundae, 215

Black Bean and Apple Salsa, 178

Blueberry Green Smoothie, 39

Brandied Peaches and Apples with Caramel Pecans, 226–27

Brie Stuffed Apples, 222

Broccoli Omelet, 66–67

Broccoli Soup, 174–75

Brussels Sprouts Casserole, 200–201

Caprese Salad with Balsamic Glaze, 101

Caramelized Onions, 155

Cauliflower Carrot Soup, 170–71

Chicken Breasts with Italian Salad, 123–25

Chicken Fajita Wraps, 110–11

Chicken Fajitas with Spicy Avocado Sauce, 130–31

Chicken Pasta Salad, 86–87

Chipotle Dip, 181

Cilantro-Lime Brown Rice, 209

Cucumber-Watermelon Cooler, 221

Curried Chicken Salad Pita Sandwich, 108–109

Delicious Bruschetta, 186–87

Delicious Oatmeal Cookies, 238–39

Diabetic-Friendly Green Smoothie, 42

Egg Burrito, 76–77

Egg Muffins, 73–74

Energy Oatmeal, 59

English Muffin with Berries, 54

Fish Tacos, 148–49

French Onion Dip, 182

Fruity Yogurt Parfait, 63

Garlicky Balsamic Vinaigrette, 93

Grandma's Guacamole, 180

Greek Salad with Lemon Vinaigrette, 100

Green Avocado Smoothie, 47

Grilled Apricots with Cinnamon, 216
Grilled Asparagus, 196
Grilled Chicken Skewers Marinated in Ginger-Apricot Sauce, 128–29
Grilled Chicken with Black Bean Salsa, 105
Grilled Collard Greens, 197
Grilled Eggplant and Zucchini, 208
Grilled Peaches with Ricotta Stuffing and Balsamic Glaze, 217
Grilled Pineapple, 218
Grilled Portobello Burger with Caramelized Onions and Pesto, 153–54
Grilled Romaine Salad with Garlicky Balsamic Vinaigrette, 95
Grilled Rustic Corn, 193
Grilled Sweet Potato Steak Fries, 194–95
Grilled Tomatillo Salsa, 102–103
Grilled Veggie Pizza, 158–59
Grown-up Berry Parfait, 235

Healthier Mac 'n' Cheese, 162–63
Healthier Stuffing, 212–13
Healthy "Lox" English Muffin, 55
Healthy Cobb Salad with Basic Vinaigrette, 96–97
Healthy French Toast, 80
Healthy Italian Pasta Salad, 88
Healthy Mini Cheesecakes with Vanilla Wafer Almond Crust, 236–37
Honey Lemon Vinaigrette, 91
Hummus Dip with Curried Pita Chips, 190–91

Insalata di Farro (Farro Salad), 82–83
Italian Herbed Turkey Cutlets, 138
Italian-Style Tuna Salad, 121
Italian Veggie Pita Sandwich, 114

Kale and Butternut Squash Sauté, 202–203
Kale Vegetable Soup, 118–19

Lemon Vinaigrette, 92

Macerated Strawberries with Homemade Whipped Cream, 228–29
Mediterranean Bowl, 156–57
Mediterranean Scramble, 72

Melon Mélange, 48
Mexican Fruit Salad, 230–31
Mexican Pizza, 160–61
Mexican Summer Salad, 94
Mini Banana Split, 234
Mini Banana Vegan Muffins, 244–45
Mom's Bean Soup, 176

Not Your Mama's Green Bean Casserole, 198–99

Open-Faced Breakfast Sandwich, 65
Orange Chicken and Brown Rice, 126–27

Pan-Steamed Orange Roughy, 146–47
Papaya Goodness, 40
Peach Green Smoothie, 46
Pinto Beans, 166–67
Plain and Simple Couscous, 210
Pomegranate Salad, 98
Protein Bowl, 56
Pumpkin Pie Smoothie, 50
Pumpkin Soup with Whole Wheat Parmesan Croutons, 168–69

Quinoa and Veggies, 211

Red Mexican Salsa, 104
Red Sangria, 219

Roasted Butternut Squash Soup, 172–73

Roasted Cauliflower, 206

Roasted Zucchini Crostini Dip, 188–89

Sautéed Greens with Cannellini Beans, 204–205

Sautéed Vegetables, 207

Sesame Salmon Fillets, 144

Spiced Applesauce, 224

Spice-Rubbed Salmon, 145

Spicy Sun-Roasted Tomato Hummus, 192

Spinach Artichoke Dip, 184–85

Strawberry Cucumber Delight, 49

Stuffed Bell Peppers, 142–43

Sweet Carrot and Apple Salad, 232

Sweet Potato Dessert, 225

Thai Curried Vegetables, 150–51

Toast with Almond Butter and Banana, 53

Tropical Salsa, 179

Tropical Smoothie, 44

Tuna Salad, 120

Turkey Chili, 115–16

Turkey Meat Loaf, 136–37

Turkey Meatballs in Marinara Sauce, 134–35

Turkey Roulade with Cider Sauce, 139–41

Tzaziki Greek Yogurt Sauce, 183

Vegan Date Nut Loaf, 240–41

Vegetarian Chili, 116–17

Veggie Fajitas, 152

Veggie Frittata with Caramelized Onions, 68–69

Veggie Omelet, 74–75

Veggie Scramble, 70

Wake Up Call!, 41

Warm Quinoa with Berries, 62

Whipped Cream, 228–29

White Sangria, 220

Whole Grain Pancakes, 78–79

Zucchini Carrot Bread, 242–43

Zucchini Muffins, 246–47

About the Authors

Dr. Mariza Snyder is an impassioned and dedicated doctor of chiropractic. She graduated from Life Chiropractic College West in Hayward, California. Her passion is to help people achieve a life of optimal health and wellness. In 2010 she published a book with Dr. Lauren Clum on nutrition called *The Antioxidant Counter: A Pocket Guide to the Revolutionary ORAC Scale for Choosing Healthy Foods*. Dr. Mariza completed her undergraduate studies at Mills College with a double degree in biology and psychology and a minor in chemistry. She currently lives in Riverside, California, and enjoys being active, traveling, reading, and educating people about health and wellness.

Dr. Lauren Clum is a chiropractor committed to helping people recognize their own healing capacities. She is the founder and director of The Specific Chiropractic Center in Oakland, California, coauthor (with Dr. Mariza Snyder) of *The Antioxidant Counter: A Pocket Guide to the Revolutionary ORAC Scale for Choosing Healthy Foods*, and part-time faculty at Life Chiropractic College West in Hayward, California. Dr. Clum completed her undergraduate degree in business administration, with an emphasis in management, at Sonoma State University in Rohnert Park, California. After graduating with honors from Life Chiropractic College West, she practiced chiropractic for a year in San Jose, Costa Rica, before returning to the Bay Area to open her current chiropractic practice.

Anna V. Zulaica is the founder and chef of Presto! Catering and Food Services. In 2009, Anna traveled to the Basque region of Spain, where she learned to cook authentic Basque dishes. She also traveled to Florence, Italy (where she took a private culinary course on Italian cuisine, wine, and the Mediterranean diet) and spent a week on an organic farm in Tuscany baking vegan breads, pastries, and biscotti in a wood-fired oven. In 2010, Anna's recipes were published in *The Antioxidant Counter: A Pocket Guide to the Revolutionary ORAC Scale for Choosing Healthy Foods.* Anna enjoys cooking and hosting for private parties in the Bay Area, as well as teaching healthy cooking classes and clinics multiple times a year. Her mission is to teach people that healthy cooking can be delicious and that eating healthy is not being on a diet, it is a lifestyle we should all follow.

Conversions

MEASURE	EQUIVALENT	METRIC
1 teaspoon	--	5 milliliters
1 tablespoon	3 teaspoons	14.8 milliliters
1 cup	16 tablespoons	236.8 milliliters
1 pint	2 cups	473.6 milliliters
1 quart	4 cups	947.2 milliliters
1 liter	4 cups + 3½ tablespoons	1000 milliliters
1 ounce (dry)	2 tablespoons	28.35 grams
1 pound	16 ounces	453.49 grams
2.21 pounds	35.3 ounces	1 kilogram
325°F/350°F/375°F/400°F	--	165°C/177°C/190°C/200°C